THE BOOK OF PRAYERS

THE BOOK

This BOOK OF PRAYERS has been compiled with the advice and counsel of the following inter-denominational advisory committee of eminent clergymen:

The Rev. WALLACE WITMER ANDERSON, D.D., formerly United Congregational Church of Bridgeport, Connecticut and Chairman of Seminar on Worship of Congregational-Christian Churches.

The Rev. GEORGE A. BUTTRICK, D.D., formerly Madison Avenue Presbyterian Church, New York City.

The Rev. PAUL SCHERER, D.D., formerly Union Theological Seminary, New York City and Minister of the Holy Trinity Lutheran Church, New York City.

The Rev. RALPH W. SOCKMAN, D.D., formerly Minister of Christ Church Methodist, New York City and Minister of the National Radio Pulpit.

The Rev. JOHN WALLACE SUTER, D.D., formerly Custodian of the Standard Book of Common Prayer and Dean of Washington Cathedral (Episcopal).

OF PRAYERS

COMPILED FOR
EVERYDAY WORSHIP

Edited by Leon and Elfreda McCauley

INTRODUCTION BY

The Rev. HARRY EMERSON FOSDICK, D.D.

Baptist. Minister-Emeritus of the Riverside Church
New York City

AVENEL BOOKS

NEW YORK

This edition is published by Avenel Books,
distributed by Crown Publishers, Inc.,
by arrangement with the author.
h g f e d c b a
AVENEL 1981 EDITION

Manufactured in the United States of America

Library of Congress Cataloging in Publication Data
Main entry under title:

The Book of prayers.

   Includes index.
   1. Prayers.   I. McCauley, Leon.   II. McCauley,
Elfreda.
BV245.B614   1981   242′.8   81-3548
ISBN: 0-517-34738-5 (Crown)   AACR2

Table of Contents

PRAYERS FOR YOUNG PEOPLE

PRAYERS FOR LITTLE CHILDREN

Preface

This book is a gathering together of helpful and personal material from the great treasuries of Protestant prayers, arranged in chapters and subdivisions so that the prayers may be readily accessible in the dark moments of personal distress. It is a book for Christians groping toward a more satisfying personal communion with their God.

This is not a scholarly book; it is not a denominational book. Nor is it a book of original prayers. Almost every one of these prayers has appeared in print before, though not always in the exact form used here. About half have been adapted to the purpose of the book, either at the suggestion of an editorial advisor or on our own initiative, in order to make them more generally useful.

Planning the book, we sought the advice of an interdenominational group of authorities on prayer—Baptist, Congregational-Christian, Episcopal, Lutheran, Methodist, Presbyterian—men representing different denominational backgrounds, men conversant with man's need to pray and his best ways of expressing prayer.

To these advisors we submitted a first draft manuscript of twelve hundred prayers, gathered from nearly one hundred collections and grouped under life-situation categories. On the manuscript the advisors were asked to indicate their reactions: what to use, what to omit, where to substitute. Approximately three-quarters of the material in the final manuscript received unanimous approval of all five advisors. That the result did not consist wholly of unanimous choices occurred only in the interest of maintaining a necessary balance in subject matter. In about one-fourth of the instances, consequently, we have used a prayer which one or another of the advisors would have omitted. Only in the case of four or five prayers did as many as two advisors have reservations, and these prayers, again, were retained solely for balance.

We have acknowledged, where known, the authors of prayers included in this volume. Published prayers are frequently regarded as public property; and anthologists have sometimes been careless about attributing to original sources the material appearing in their volumes. When we do not have an author's name, we have credited the prayer to the earliest published collection, accessible to us, in which it appears, or to the collection in which the adaptation we have used appears; but in neither case is the material necessarily original to that source.

We are beyond words grateful to the advisory group —Drs. Wallace Witmer Anderson, George A. Buttrick, Paul Scherer, Ralph W. Sockman, and John Wallace Suter—for their thoughtful advice and aid; and to Dr. Harry Emerson Fosdick for his introductory essay. Without the help of these men, there could have been no book. The comfort and help it may bring to men today—that is their contribution; its weaknesses, its shortcomings—these are our responsibility.

THE EDITORS

The Strength of Personal Prayer

AN INTRODUCTION

By Harry Emerson Fosdick

Nothing more deeply intimate can be conceived than the genuine prayer of an individual soul. "Spirit of God, descend upon my heart"—each person must pray that for himself and there can be no proxies. Nevertheless, other souls also have prayed and have left the record of their communion with God, and these written prayers that sprang from the depths of great spirits, bringing them "authentic tidings of invisible things" and releasing in them power to do what they ought to do and to stand what they must endure, can be of incalculable help to each of us. This book is published with the hope that it may bring to many people inspiration and guidance in their own private praying.

A troubled generation like ours, that makes a heavy demand on our resources, calls for prayer. Action, output, work—to this strenuous side of our lives our era appeals. It fairly shouts at us about duties, responsibilities, obligations. Yes, but a tree must have deep roots if it is to have strong branches. Even an airplane, with all its powers of flight and speed, is useless without ground service. The more the output, the greater the need of replenishment and intake—that is law universal, nowhere more manifest than in personal experience. Anyone who in a time like this hears only the call to go all out is sure in the end to find himself all in.

Our situation today, therefore, little as it outwardly may seem to do so, leads our thought straight into the realm of prayer, and that, too, by a route that should make the matter personally cogent. In quiet, easy days we may approach prayer speculatively, arguing our different theories about it, but today to multitudes of us prayer is not primarily a matter of theory but of *need*. We are in exigent want of intake to match output. If prayer means power, resource, fresh faith, and renewed courage, as the great exemplars of prayers have said it does, then we must have it somehow or other. A speculative sceptic may argue that prayer is theoretically irrational but, all the time he is talking, one keeps thinking of some hard-hitting, hard-living man, like Henry M. Stanley, coming out of his terrific experience in Africa, and saying: "On all my expeditions prayer made me stronger, morally and mentally, than any of my non-praying companions. It did not blind my eyes, or dull my mind, or close my ears; but, on the contrary, it gave me confidence. It did more; it gave me joy and pride in my work, and lifted me hopefully over the one thousand five hundred miles of forest tracks, eager to face the day's perils and fatigues." What we want to know is: what is that strength-giving resource? Never mind the theory now or even the name one calls it by —what is that power and how does one get it? Prayer, like food, is most vitally approached when one is in hungry need of it.

Luke's gospel tells us that on the critical day when Jesus told his disciples once for all that the Cross confronted him, he prayed; and "As he was praying, the fashion of his countenance was altered." Perhaps he, too, had looked tense and drawn, harassed and fearful. Perhaps even his face had revealed his inner struggle. But while he was praying, so Moffatt translates the verse, "the appearance of his face altered." Faith for fear, strength for anxiety, confidence for hesitation, inward power adequate for whatever peril—that change showed in his face. If such an experience is possible, we of this generation certainly need it.

The prayers in this book are intimate, spiritual autobiography. They take us into the depths of human souls, confessing their sins, voicing their thankfulness, seeking guidance in their confusion and resource in their inadequacy, sometimes resting back on the "everlasting arms," and sometimes with ardent desire presenting their petitions. Biography can tell us the outward events of a man's life—as, for example, Martin Luther's con-

frontation of the Emperor at Worms with his uncom-
promising courage, "Here I stand! I cannot do otherwise"—but only autobiography can reveal what was
going on inside the man. Fortunately Luther told us
that. He was praying. As he faced the Emperor, he said:
"O Thou my God, stand by me against all the world.
Do thou do it! Thou must do it! Thou alone! It is
indeed not my cause but thine." It takes such a man's
prayers to explain him. They come from the intimate
depths and, whether in life's common days or in momentous crises like Luther's, they can be drums and
bugles in the soul.

In this introduction I shall try simply to point out
some of the characteristic qualities of genuine communion with God, revealed in the prayers which this
book contains.

For one thing, a shift of attitude from the aggressiveness of daily life to spiritual quietness, openness, hospitality is almost always present. There are two aspects
to every strong life—rootage and fruitage, receptivity
and activity, relaxation and tension, resting back and
working hard. A man who cannot do the former can
never do the latter well, never! He who cannot rest,
cannot work; he who cannot let go, cannot hold on; he
who cannot find footing, cannot go forward. The offices
of psychiatrists are littered with folk who have mas-
tered the techniques of activity and aggressiveness and

now are going all to pieces because they have failed to master that other technique: they have nothing to rest back upon.

Listen to this prayer from the great tradition of the Church: "Let my soul take refuge from the crowding turmoil of worldly thoughts beneath the shadow of thy wings; let my heart, this sea of restless waves, find peace in thee, O God." Whose prayer was that? Saint Augustine's. A weak man? One of history's momentous characters, from his early struggles with himself until at last, after an immeasurably important contribution to the world, as Bishop of Hippo in North Africa, he fell on sleep while the invading barbarians were at the city's gates and the Roman empire was tumbling down about his ears. There is no understanding such a life without such prayer. He had something to rest back upon.

There are two ways to learn to pray. One is to try to argue it all out first, solve all the theoretical difficulties, and then, having our questions answered and our doubts resolved, say, "Now I will try to pray." That method seldom issues in profound experience. But one often sees another kind of thing happen—sees folk who started with the need of backing greater than their own, the desperate need of it, and who, theory or no theory, reached out for God and found him there, found some power indubitably there that they could rest back upon, so that now they faced all gainsayers with a first-hand experience no speculative argument could confute. Prayer is real. "Strengthened with might by his Spirit in the inner man"—that is real!

On the Maine coast a boy asked an old sailor, "What is the wind?" and after a long pause the old man answered, "I don't know. I can't tell you. But I know how to hoist a sail." To some reader we hope this book will say: Try prayer, will you? Endless unanswered questions yet about the wind, but still the wind is real. Hoist your sail, and see!

Another factor is characteristic of Christian prayer at its best—affirmation, positive affirmation of faith and confidence in God that puts divine strength in the center of the picture and crowds apprehensions, anxieties, and fears off the edge. Who does not face hours when doubts and dismays, worries and apprehensions crowd up into the center of his mind? How obsessing such hours can be! And when they come, something must be done about it. Even the Master had such hours. Did he not cry once, "Now is my soul troubled; and what shall I say?" Did he not in Gethsemane exclaim, "My soul is exceedingly sorrowful, even unto death"? But then he prayed, and confidence and courage marched in; the great convictions that sustained him and the great resources that supported him moved up into the center of his soul.

[6]

The Strength of Personal Prayer

Real prayer is always more than begging; it is affirmation:

Though I walk through the valley of the
    shadow of death,
I will fear no evil; for thou art with me—

that is prayer.

I . . . am persuaded that he is able to keep that
    which I have committed unto him against that day—

that is prayer. It carries up into the center of the soul convictions and reassurances that crowd out apprehensions and fears.

John Bunyan wrote *Pilgrim's Progress* in Bedford jail. Anxieties crowded up on him—for himself, yes, but more for his family, and especially for that blind child of his whom he most dearly loved. It was his own personal experience he was describing when he wrote about Apollyon, the foul fiend, who "stradled quite over the whole breadth of the way, and said, 'Prepare thy self to die, for I swear by my Infernal Den, that thou shalt go no further, here will I spill thy soul.' " Nevertheless, Bunyan's soul was not spilled; no, nor countless others' who have known his inner secret. Prayers can blow trumpets in one's spirit. An old legend says that after the angels had rebelled in heaven and had been cast out into their eternal prison, they were asked what they missed most and they answered, "The sound of the trumpets in the morning." *That* is prayer!

Another factor in the great praying of the Christian heritage is the experience of daily, continuous, divine companionship in which at its best prayer issues. We can choose our interior spiritual company—in that brief statement lies a truth that could remake our lives. Many things in the outer world we cannot choose; there we are the victims of necessity, and during these days in particular we have to live in much depressing company. But within ourselves we can choose our spiritual companionship. There we are masters of our hospitality. There we can live in a great and stimulating fellowship.

Prayer is establishing ourselves "in a sense of God's presence by continually conversing with him." Who said that? Brother Lawrence, a medieval Catholic saint. Prayer is making "frequent colloquies, or short discoursings, between God and thy own soul." Who said that? Jeremy Taylor, a Protestant leader of the seventeenth century. This thing we are saying now is no modern thinning out of prayer but the essence of prayer's meaning as the great souls of the Church have experienced it: the maintenance of an habitual, spiritual fellowship.

We talk much today about practical Christianity. Good! Christianity that feeds the hungry, clothes the naked, and works for social reformation; the Christianity of the Good Samaritan serving those of whom Jesus said, "Inasmuch as ye have done it unto one of the least of these my brethren, ye have done it unto me"—such Christianity calls for fruit on the tree; it wants practical results. Right! But the tree's roots are practical, too, critically practical, and watching modern Christians one is concerned about that aspect of the matter. "He shall be like a tree," says the Psalmist, "planted by the streams of water that bringeth forth its fruit in its season." Many of us need that double emphasis. Even the Master's life reached the place where all his stress on practical service would not fill the bill. For all of that he would have been long since forgotten; what saw him through was something underground, not visible to the eye, his rootage, "a tree planted by the streams of water."

This aspect of the Master's life and of our own involves the companionship we live in. Thank God for our friends! When the Master's face was transfigured he too was in the company of his friends. But there was more to it than that. Even when his friends failed him and the world turned on him a forbidding face, he still had stimulating companionship within.

It was my privilege to know a woman who in her early middle years was left a widow with five children and who resolutely shouldered the practical and spiritual responsibilities which that entailed. By careful management she saw the children through college. On the day of her burial, in her ninety-sixth year, one of the children said he had never seen her, even in the most troubled times, distraught to the point of giving up. One son became president of a great railway system, another became president of a state university, another distinguished himself in medical research. That kind of mother is no accident. It was the university president who said to me that no one could understand her who did not understand her prayer-life. It was a strong, sustaining force, he said; her resource came from an unfailing, inward companionship.

To be sure, there are misuses of prayer, and many souls have been estranged from praying and deprived of its consolations and reinforcements because they have seen so much superstition and self-seeking mingled with it. Prayer is not a magic way of getting things without fulfilling the conditions of getting them. Prayer is not a process by which mortal man turns eternal God into a bell-boy to run his errands. Prayer is not an emergency measure by which men who otherwise seldom think of God get themselves out of tight places. Prayer is not an ivory tower, a place of soft retreat, to which cowardly souls merely run away to escape from life. Such misuses of prayer are its perversions and caricatures. In the genuine Christian heritage, God, to those who knew the deep meanings of prayer, has been an unseen Friend, an invisible Companion. When they were alone, they were never alone. Then, when emergency came, they traveled an accustomed road, like Jesus in Gethsemane, to a familiar Presence for a brief colloquy, to emerge again ready to face the wrath of devils and the scorn of men. As one English churchman put it, his prayers had for the most part resolved themselves into two words: "Now, Lord!"

This leads to a climactic fact about the experience of Christian prayer: it releases superhuman power. It gets things done which otherwise would not be done. As Alexis Carrel, the scientist, said, "When we pray, we link ourselves with the inexhaustible motive power that spins the universe." At this point modern science provides a cogent analogy to prayer's meaning. Our dictionaries only a few years ago were defining "uranium" as "a rare, heavy, white metallic element... has no important uses." So! Uranium had no important uses! But it has now shaken the world to its foundations, because science has released its power. Such is the task of science in the physical realm—to fulfil conditions that release power; and in the realm of the spirit that is prayer's effect, too.

Christian prayer is not the endeavor to get God to do what we want. Christian prayer is the endeavor to put ourselves into such relationships with God that he can do, in and for and through us, what he wants. All the worst misunderstandings and perversions of prayer start with egotism—ourselves at the center and we endeavoring to get God to do our will. But Jesus' prayer started at the other end—God first, what he wants predominant, and prayer opening up the way for the release of his purpose, giving gangway to his action and free course to his power: "Not my will, but thine, be done." Without such prayer God can never do in, and for, and through us, what he wants to do.

Try teaching music to a child who does not want to learn music! This is a baffling task. The whole world of music here, and you, more than willing to share it with the child, are frustrated and estopped, for this simple reason—there is no prayer for music in the child. A recent book by a schoolteacher remarks that trying to teach an unresponsive youth makes one "understand what a dynamo feels like when it is discharging into a non-conductor." I should think God would feel like that—his dynamic will waiting to be done, but how can it be discharged into non-conductors? Without prayer there are some things God cannot say to us, for prayer is the listening ear. Without prayer, there are some things God cannot give to us, for prayer is the hospitable heart. Without prayer, there are some things God cannot do through us, for prayer is the cooperative will.

Prayer, therefore, is not merely a subjective psychological experience without objective consequence. The most tremendous objective consequences on earth come from released power. Even in the physical world we do not, by our science, create power; we release it, with momentous results. So, when David Livingstone prayed about Africa: "May God in mercy permit me to do something for the cause of Christ in these dark places of the earth!" he did not change God's intention but he did change God's action. He did not alter God's purpose but he did release it. There was a fresh invasion of the world by God through Livingstone. Who can set limits to the possibilities of that?

For such praying these present days do call. For action, yes—determined, courageous, tireless action—but all the more because of that, for those interior resources that only great praying can supply.

The Lord's Prayer
— For Every Man

Our Father, who art in heaven,
   Hallowed be thy Name.
   Thy kingdom come.
   Thy will be done,
On earth as it is in heaven.
Give us this day our daily bread.
And forgive us our trespasses,
As we forgive those who trespass against us.
And lead us not into temptation,
But deliver us from evil.
For thine is the kingdom, and the power, and the glory,
For ever and ever. Amen.

Prayers for Adults

I.

Daily Prayers

IN THE MORNING

O God, most holy, wise, and powerful preserver and governor of all thy creatures and all their actions: Keep us this day in health of body and soundness of mind, in purity of heart and cheerfulness of spirit, in contentment with our lot and charity with our neighbor; and further all our lawful undertakings with thy blessing. In our labor strengthen us, in our pleasure purify us, in our difficulties direct us, in our perils defend us, in our troubles comfort us, and supply all our needs; according to the riches of thy grace in Christ Jesus our Lord. Amen.

O Lord, our heavenly Father, almighty and everlasting God, who hast safely brought us to the beginning of this day: Defend us in the same with thy mighty power; and grant that this day we fall into no sin, neither run into any kind of danger; but that all our doings may be ordered by thy governance, to do always what is righteous in thy sight; through Jesus Christ our Lord. Amen.

O God, who orderest all things in heaven and earth: Help me to go about the tasks and duties of this day with the remembrance that I am thy servant therein. Make me honest, painstaking, and cheerful, and grant that all I do and say may bring good to others and glory to thy holy Name; through Jesus Christ our Lord. Amen.

O Lord, let my first thoughts be of thee; to praise and to thank thee for thy goodness and thy protection through the night. Give me thy grace, I pray thee, so to live through this day that at nightfall I may not be ashamed to meet thee; for Jesus' sake. Amen.

I thank thee, O God, for keeping me through the night, and for the promise of this new day. I would begin it with thee and pray that it may be to me a day of growth in the spirit and of service for thee and thy kingdom in the world. Help me to meet with quiet confidence whatever trials the day holds for me; strengthen me against temptation; and keep me always loyal to our Lord and Saviour Jesus Christ. Amen.

Daily Prayers

In the name of God the Father, Son, and Holy Ghost: I thank thee, my heavenly Father, through Jesus Christ, thy dear Son, that thou hast kept me this night from all harm and danger; and I pray thee that thou wouldst keep me this day also from sin and every evil, that all my doings and life may please thee. For into thy hands I commend myself, my body and soul, and all things. Let thy holy angel be with me that the wicked foe may have no power over me. Amen.

AT NOON

Give peace for all time, O Lord, and fill my heart and the hearts of all men everywhere with the spirit of our Lord Jesus Christ. Amen.

At this half-tide between night and night, do thou, O Lord of light, bridge the darkness of my sin with the brightness of thy glory, giving thy grace that I may greet the evening in thy continued presence; for Jesus' sake. Amen.

IN THE EVENING

Send thy peace into my heart, O Lord, that I may be contented with thy mercies of this day and confident of thy protection for this night; and having forgiven others, even as thou dost forgive me, may I go to my rest in tranquility and trust; through Jesus Christ our Lord. Amen.

[17]

O thou whose chosen dwelling is the heart that longs for thy presence and humbly seeks thy face: We come to thee as the day declines and the shadows fall. Deepen within us a sense of shame and sorrow for the wrongs we have done, for the good we have left undone; and strengthen every desire to amend our lives according to thy holy will. Restore unto us the joy of thy salvation; bind up that which is broken; give light to our minds, strength to our wills, and rest to our souls; according to thy loving kindness in Jesus Christ our Lord. Amen.

Be present, O merciful God, and protect us through the silent hours of this night, so that we who are wearied by the work and the changes of this fleeting world may rest upon thy eternal changlessness; through Jesus Christ our Lord. Amen.

Almighty God, whose voice is best heard not in earthquake or wind or fire but in the stillness of our prayers, speak now in silence; and so grant us the gift of thy Spirit that our restless spirits may find peace— and then share thy peace.

We come burdened by failure. Yet the burden proves that we are made of thee for better things. We have been sharp tongued when we should have been patient and falsely patient when we should have spoken a brave word. We have been swift to blame our world and all too slow and blind to our own faults. We have been content while the heavenly vision has faded into the light of common day. We have lived as though Christ had never lived or died or broken the bonds of death. Now we come home to thee because we are tired of ourselves. Receive us, we pray, despite all our undeserving, and cleanse us, and give us a new heart.

We come with praises on our lips. How little we can do or earn; how much thou hast given! We cannot make seedtime and harvest, or grace of simple friendship, or the prophet's word, or the coming of Christ, or the life everlasting! Yet these thou dost give, good measure, pressed down, running over! Keep us from the shabbiness of our complaints, deepen our gratitude, and teach us to live among our fellows with glad love.

We come with prayers in behalf of all men. We pray thee to guide and guard this nation and all peoples, to bless men in their toil and to sustain thy Church. We pray for the sick and for the untroubled, for friend and for foe, for strangers and for those we love. Thus praying, we claim thy promise that as our days so shall our strength be—until we reach thy shining country where beyond these voices there is peace. For we pray in Christ's name. Amen.

II.
Of Country Life

THANKSGIVING FOR THIS WORLD

O God, we thank thee for this universe, our great home, for its vastness and its riches, and for the manifoldness of the life which teems upon it and of which we are part. We praise thee for the arching sky and the blessed winds, for the driving clouds and the constellations on high. We praise thee for the salt sea and the running water, for the everlasting hills, for the trees, and for the grass under our feet. We thank thee for our senses by which we can see the splendor of the morning, hear the jubilant songs of love, and smell the breath of the springtime. Grant us, we pray thee, a heart wide open to all this joy and beauty, and save our souls from being so steeped in care or so darkened by passion that we pass heedless and unseeing when even the thornbush by the wayside is aflame with the glory of God. Amen.

FOR A GOOD USE OF THE EARTH

Blessed Lord, who hast given us the earth to live on, warmed by the sun, made wet by the rain, having fields and gardens and orchards: Help us to use these good things fairly, and with kindness one toward another, working for each other and living for thee. Glory be to thee, O Lord. Amen.

FOR KINDNESS TO ANIMALS

Almighty and most merciful Father, the Father of our Lord Jesus Christ, and our Father, the Creator of all life: We remember before thee with thanksgiving thy creatures that are upon the earth, and in the sea, and in the air. Grant that we, having power over them, may learn to use it with mercy. May we never exploit them for selfish ends but seek in all our dealings with them to succor the weak and the helpless. As they contribute to the beauty and labor of the world, so may we increase that beauty and fulfill that labor, that all creation may praise and glorify thee for ever. Amen.

FOR A BLESSING ON FARMERS

O eternal God, thou Lord of springtime and harvest, bless, we pray thee, those who sow the seed and reap the harvest. Grant that they may enjoy not only the fruits of the earth but those of the Spirit, love and joy and peace; through Jesus Christ our Lord. Amen.

FOR FIELDS AND CROPS

O Lord our God, author and giver of all good things, who hast ordained the earth to bring forth grass for cattle, and herbs and food for the services of man:

The Book of Prayers

Look down in thy compassion upon us, and bless, we beseech thee, the labors of thy servants who till and sow the fields. Vouchsafe to us seasonable weather; cause thy sun to shine, and let thy rain and dew refresh the ground, that there may be abundance of food, both for man and for beast. So we thy people and the sheep of thy pasture will give thee thanks for ever; we will show forth thy praise to all generations; through the same Jesus Christ our Lord. Amen.

Beautiful Saviour, King of Creation, we thank thee for thy power and majesty as it governs the growing things in our fields. Teach us, dear Lord, that we work for thee in supplying, in due season, the needs of our fellow-men for bread. Preserve us from all selfishness, all pride, all dishonor to thee. Give us diligence and skill in raising and gathering our harvests. Protect our fields from all sudden destruction, and let the earth yield its increase. If it be thy good will to grant us plenty, quicken our hearts to share with such as are in need. If it should be thy purpose to afflict us in our labors, prepare us even now to meet the test of faith. Make us thankful to thee for the joy of working amid growing things, and open our eyes to the glories of thy handiwork. Teach us to seek first thy kingdom and the righteousness which our Saviour has provided, and then all else shall be added unto us. Grant that the fruits of the field may find such distribution that buyer and seller be properly benefited. These gifts we ask of thee because thou art the giver of all things for body and for soul. Amen.

Almighty God, who hast blessed the earth that it should be fruitful and bring forth whatsoever is needful for the life of man, and hast commanded us to work with quietness, and eat our own bread: Bless the labors of the husbandman and grant such seasonable weather that we may gather in the fruits of the earth, and ever rejoice in thy goodness, to the praise of thy holy Name; through Jesus Christ our Lord. Amen.

THANKSGIVING FOR THE HARVEST

O Lord God Almighty, the Creator and Father of all: We yield thee hearty thanks that thou hast ordained for mankind both seedtime and harvest and dost now bestow upon us thy children the fruits of the earth in their season. For these and all other of thy mercies we laud and magnify thy glorious Name; through Jesus Christ our Lord. Amen.

Most gracious God: We yield thee unfeigned thanks and praise for the return of seedtime and harvest, for the increase of the ground and the gathering in of the fruits thereof, and for all the other blessings of thy merciful providence bestowed upon this nation and people. And, we beseech thee, give us a just sense of these great mercies; such as may appear in our lives by an humble, holy, and obedient walking before thee all our days; through Jesus Christ our Lord, to whom, with thee and the Holy Ghost, be all glory and honor, world without end. Amen.

FOR SPIRITUAL HARVESTS

Lord of seedtime and harvest, bless, we beseech thee, the toil of the farmer. Give him joy in his task and the vision, beyond his furrow, of bread enough and to spare. Teach us anew, from thy fields, the meanings of the harvest of the soul. Soften our hearts to the hearing of the Master's word and discipline our wayward wills to fruitful obedience. Amen.

III.

Of a Woman's World

OF WORK ABOUT THE HOME

O Lord, I pray thee to bless all that I do this day. Accept it as an act of worship and give me grace to find thee in every task and duty, however small or dull it may sometimes be. Amen.

O Father, light up the small duties of this day's life. May they shine with the beauty of thy countenance. May we believe that glory may dwell in the commonest task. For the sake of Jesus Christ our Lord, we ask it. Amen.

AFTER BREAKFAST

O God, thou Father of us all, this is the hour when in my day there comes a lull; breakfast is over, my husband has gone to his work, and I have helped the children into their rubbers and their coats and off to school. And now I have closed the door and find myself alone. O God, go with them all; beyond my sight and voice they live and move, but not beyond thy care. Guide these precious ones of mine. Keep them from those things that make us weak and lesser souls. I pray in the Name of thine own Son, our Lord and Saviour Jesus Christ. Amen.

FOR PATIENCE WITH SMALL CHILDREN

O Jesus Christ, you called little children to you. My little ones are continually underfoot, with endless questions and demands. But help me not to be impatient. Help me to remember how few are these years of dependence, how soon these children will go their way without me. May I find joy in them every day, and be glad of the chances, which their constant presence brings me, to guide them.

O God, in the midst of turmoil and confusion, when a dozen things must be done at once, when the children are excited or fractious and I am at the breaking point, wilt thou reach forth a steadying hand. May I find again that in quietness and confidence shall be my strength. May laughter come with its saving grace, laughter which rises from a heart at peace with thee. Amen.

BEFORE GOING SHOPPING

Help me, O God, to spend wisely and to buy fairly, remembering that money and the things of this world are a trust for which I shall have to give an account to thee. Amen.

Of a Woman's World

BEFORE ENTERTAINING GUESTS

O Lord, I pray thee ever to be my first guest, that my friends may find thee in my home. Give us thy gift of happy friendship, and do thou control our thoughts and words by thy blessed presence. Amen.

FOR BEING EQUAL TO LIFE'S TASKS

Give us grace, O Lord, to work while it is day, fulfilling diligently and patiently whatever duty thou appointest us, doing small things in the day of small things and great labors if thou summon us to any. Go with me, and I will go; but if thou go not with me, send me not; let me hear thy voice when I follow. Amen.

FOR TRANQUILITY

O Lord, this is all my desire—to walk along the path of life thou hast appointed me, in steadfastness of faith, in meekness of spirit, in loneliness of heart, in gentleness of love. And because outward events have such power to scatter my thoughts and disturb the inward peace in which alone I can hear thy Spirit, do thou, gracious Lord, calm and settle my soul by that power which alone can bring all thoughts and desires into captivity to thyself. Do thou with all I have as seems best to thee, for I know not what is best. Let not the cares or duties of this life press on me too heavily but lighten my burden that I may follow in thy way in quietness, filled with thankfulness for thy mercy and rendering acceptable service unto thee. Amen.

Keep us from inner anger, O Lord, so that our words and deeds may not hinder those who depend upon us for encouragement and strength. Nurture truth and generosity in us and keep us in the light of thy Presence. Amen.

FOR A PURPOSEFUL LIFE

When we have found life good, O Lord, we have asked for longer days; when we have found it heavy, we have asked for a lighter load. Teach us to accept whatever comes to us as useful cargo freighted with possible blessing. Help us to wrest a blessing from circumstance, to work with thee in making all things work together for good because we will to live according to thy purpose. Amen.

FOR HARMONIOUS LIVING

Our Father, give us, we pray thee, eyes to see and ears to hear; give us open minds and gentle hearts. Keep us indifferent to time and place but keenly aware of the simple human values by means of which men, women, and children live happily together. In Jesus' Name. Amen.

Of a Woman's World

FOR TACT

O Lord, who art full of love and mercy, help me to be careful of the feelings of others. Let me beware of the hasty word, the prying question, and the indelicate allusion that hurt worse than a blow. Show me how to put the shy at ease, and to give them confidence by words of kindness and true interest in them. Keep me from blundering into the sacred places of others. Give me a wholesome sense of the rights of others, that I may not even seem to disregard them. Bestow on me keen insight, that I may see at once the fitting thing to do. For Jesus' sake. Amen.

IV.

Of Parenthood

FOR CHILDREN

O Lord Jesus Christ, who didst take little children into thine arms and bless them: Bless, we beseech thee, the children of this family, grant that they may grow up in thy fear and love; give unto them day by day thy strength and guidance, that so they may continue in thy love and service unto their lives' end. Grant this, O blessed Saviour, for thine own Name's sake. Amen.

Almighty God and heavenly Father, we thank thee for the children whom thou hast given us. Give us also grace to train them in thy faith, fear, and love, that as they advance in years they may grow in grace and may hereafter be found in the number of thine elect children; through Jesus Christ our Lord. Amen.

Let my love, O God, be freely given to my child and let me never cloak in loving words demands of selfishness or pride, but let me, ever loving *him*, commend *him* to thy greater love, wherein is perfect freedom; through Jesus Christ our Lord. Amen.

Of Parenthood

ON THE EXPECTATION OF A CHILD

O God, the giver of all good gifts, we praise and thank thee for this gift of new life and the power to create life. Thou hast allowed us to join with thee in the creation of a human personality with an eternal soul. Prepare us in thine own way for the receiving of the child thou hast entrusted to us that it may be duly brought up in the light and love of thy Son Jesus Christ our Lord. Amen.

OF THANKSGIVING FOR A CHILD

We thank thee, O God, our Father, for this our child. Help us as true disciples to set *him* a good example in all we think or say or do, keep *him* well in body and mind, and grant that *he* may grow in grace and in the knowledge and love of thy Son, our Saviour Jesus Christ. Amen.

AT THE BEDSIDE OF A CHILD

Be with this thy child, O heavenly Father, during the night. Grant *him* a quiet night, a peaceful rest, and a new day to grow in thy grace and to increase in stature and favor with thee. Amen.

ON THE ADOPTION OF A CHILD

Our Father, who hast bestowed upon us this great privilege of taking to ourselves, as one of our own, one of thy little ones, to love and care for and to bring up in thy faith and fear: Grant us, we pray thee, the grace to give to *him* the full measure of our devotion and to set before *him* always a good example of Christian life. Bless us in our growth together, and may our home be enriched in the simple joys that come of loving and serving one another; through Jesus Christ our Lord. Amen.

AT A BAPTISM

Lord Jesus, friend of children, we have brought our child, precious to thee, to holy baptism that *he* may be thine now and throughout eternity. Thou hast through this blessed sacrament received *him* into thine everlasting arms of love. Bless *him* and keep *him* from every danger of body and soul.

Grant that *he* may be faithful to thee who hast redeemed *him* with thine own precious blood. And at last bring *him* with us all to the eternal home in heaven to live in thy presence forevermore. Amen.

OF FATHERHOOD

Help me, O God, so to live that this my child may not be shamed by me; so to give *him* of my time and of myself that mutual joy may abound and multiply; and so to honor *him* as thine that I may build no willful prison round about *him*, but may free *him* in thy perfect will and care; through Jesus Christ our Lord. Amen.

OF MOTHERHOOD

Most loving God, because there are those who look up to me, I would look up to thee. They trust me, and I need thy help that I may not fail their trust. They learn from me, and I need to be enlightened so that what they learn may be only what is right and true. They think that in my love they find their security. But where can we find this security in love but in thee? For all love is thy gift, since thou art love, and thou wilt help us as we try to live in thee. Amen.

ON A BIRTHDAY

O God, I come to thee with a heart full of thankfulness for my child and all that *he* means to our family. As I watch with joy *his* growth in height and vigor, may I be able to help *him* grow also in favor with thee and man. As *he* learns more of Jesus Christ and responds to him with loyalty, may Christ's championship of the weak, Christ's willingness to suffer for doing the right, Christ's concern to find and do thy will, become a part of my child's very being. May *he* join us, *his* parents, in fuller discipleship to the Son of God, as *he* goes forth to fight against all that is wrong in us and in the world. Amen.

AS CHILDREN LEAVE FOR SCHOOL

O Lord of love, watch over these children who are dear to me. They go where I cannot follow or counsel them. They face temptations from which I cannot save them. Be thou within their hearts, their companion and guide. Give them strength to be honest. Give them grace to be kind. Grant them courage to stand up for the right, whatever the consequences. When they return may I be prepared to listen to the story of their day with sympathy and understanding. May I not expect too much of them, nor too little. Make me able to rejoice in their successes, share their griefs, and love them through everything, as thou dost love us all, O blessed Lord. Amen.

FOR AN ERRING CHILD

O God, I bring to thee my concern over my child. Thou knowest my grief as I see *him* stray from thy ways and refuse guidance and help. If I have failed in understanding *him*, if I have lacked the wisdom of love, show me how I may learn wherein I have erred, and give me the strength I need to do better.

Remembering thy never-ending patience with me and with all thy children, may I not lose heart. May my steadfast love and readiness to forgive remind *him* of the one who will never fail *him* or desert *him*. If *he* must learn one of life's hard lessons by enduring the consequences of *his* wrongdoing, may *he* see even this as one way in which love manifests itself. In the Name of Jesus Christ and his redeeming love, I pray. Amen.

FOR A SON OR DAUGHTER IN THE ARMED FORCES

O God of mercy, be with our beloved ———— in all times of temptation or peril, of boredom or weariness, of loneliness or suffering. Wherever *his* lot is cast, may *he* be conscious of an unseen presence, of thy unfailing concern for *him* and for every man. Give *him* also a deep unconquerable joy. In spite of all the sin and stupidity and cruelty of men, assure *him* that this is thy world and that the ultimate outcome of all things will be in accord with thy wisdom and thy will. So may the peace which the world cannot give fill *his* heart and *his* mind in Jesus Christ. Amen.

V.

Of Home and Family

Visit, we beseech thee, most gracious Father, this family and household with thy protection. Let thy blessing descend and rest on all who belong to it. Guide us here, and hereafter bring us to thy glory; through Jesus Christ our Lord. Amen.

Almighty God, who art the author of all goodness, look down in mercy upon this family and household and bless all who belong to it, present or absent. Save and defend us in all dangers and adversities, give us all things that are needful for our souls and bodies, and bring us safely to thy heavenly kingdom; through Jesus Christ our Lord. Amen.

Almighty God, our heavenly Father, who settest the solitary in families, we commend to thy continual care the homes in which thy people dwell. Put far from them, we beseech thee, every root of bitterness, the desire of vain glory, and the pride of life. Fill them with faith, virtue, knowledge, temperance, patience, godliness. Knit together in constant affection those who, in holy wedlock, have been made one; turn the heart of parents to the children, and the heart of the children to the parents; and so kindle charity among us all that we be evermore kindly affectioned with brotherly love; through Jesus Christ our Lord. Amen.

O almighty God, we thank thee for all thy blessings and all thy mercies which thou in thy love hast bestowed upon us. Do thou continue thy care for us. Help us to live as thine obedient and dutiful children. Let us never forget who thou art and whose we are; and grant to every member of this house strength and courage for the battle of life; for the sake of Jesus Christ our Lord. Amen.

O God, bless our home, our family, friends, and neighbors, and give us thankful hearts for all thy mercies. Amen.

FOR RELATIVES AND FRIENDS

Almighty God, we entrust all who are dear to us to thy never-failing care and love, for this life and the life to come, knowing that thou art doing for them better things than we can desire or pray for; through Jesus Christ our Lord. Amen.

FOR THOSE WITHOUT FAMILY

O God, who settest the solitary in families, we pray for all who are without children or kin. Relate them in life with those who need their strength and love, and make them one in the fellowship of the Spirit, in the Church of thy dear Son. Amen.

FOR ONE LEAVING HOME

O God, who art the strength and the protector of thy people, we humbly place in thy hands the member of this family who is today about to leave us and enter a new sphere of life and work. Keep and preserve *him*, O Lord, as it seemeth best to thy divine wisdom and love, in all health and safety, both of body and soul; through Jesus Christ our Lord. Amen.

FOR ABSENT LOVED ONES

Lord, gracious and merciful, who watchest even over the sparrows and dost uphold all things in thine everlasting arms, protect and keep our absent loved ones. Watch thou over them tenderly that no evil come nigh to them as we are separated one from another.

Keep them faithful to thy Word and thy Church. Guard and protect them as they are tempted by the allurements of sin and the unbelief of the world.

Keep them pure in heart and clean in mind and healthy in body. Dwell in them day by day. Abide with us and with them and bring them safely home to us and at last to the eternal home in heaven. Then thine shall be the glory, thine the praise, world without end; through Jesus Christ our Lord. Amen.

Of Home and Family

FOR A FAMILY BIRTHDAY

We thank thee, heavenly Father, for all thy mercies during the years that are past, and pray for thy continued blessing through the days to come. As thou hast been mindful of us, so make us always mindful of thee. Our times are in thy hand, and thou art our hope and strength. Do thou, we beseech thee, abide with us, guide and keep us, until at last we come to thine everlasting kingdom; through Jesus Christ our Lord. Amen.

FOR A MARRIAGE

O God, who out of all the world hast let us find one another and learn together the meaning of love, let us never fail to hold love precious. Let the flame of it never grow dim but burn in our hearts as an unwavering devotion and shine through our eyes in gentleness and understanding. As the road of life we walk together lengthens, forbid that the dust of it should ever drift into our souls. Help us to have the sense to climb high places of memory and imagination, so that we may remember the beauty that lies behind us and believe in the beauty that lies before. Make us sure that romance does not depend on time or place but that daily it may be renewed in the recognition of those larger possibilities which love itself creates. Teach us to remember the little courtesies, to be swift to speak the grateful and the happy word, to believe rejoicingly in each other's best, and to face all life bravely because we face it with united hearts. So may whatever spot of earth thou givest us to dwell in be as a garden in which all sweet and lovely things may grow; through Jesus Christ our Lord. Amen.

ON A WEDDING ANNIVERSARY

Heavenly Father, we give thee heartfelt thanks, on this anniversary of the day when we were made one in holy matrimony, for thy blessing upon us then and for thy continual mercies until now. We thank thee that our love has deepened with the passing days and for all the joys of our home and family life. Renew thy blessing upon us now, we beseech thee, as we renew our vows of love and loyalty, and may thy Holy Spirit strengthen us that we may ever remain steadfast in our faith and in thy service; through Jesus Christ our Lord. Amen.

VI.
Family Graces

We thank thee, our heavenly Father, for thy care over us, and pray that thou wilt bless this food to our use. Amen.

O God our Father, who givest food for the body and truth for the mind, so enlighten and nourish us that we may grow wise and strong to do thy will. Amen.

For these and all his blessings, God's holy Name be praised; through Jesus Christ our Lord. Amen.

Lord, make us truly grateful for the blessings of this day and keep us thine forevermore. Amen.

For this our daily bread and for every good gift which cometh down from thee, we bless thy holy Name; through Jesus Christ our Lord. Amen.

Bless, O Lord, this food to our use and us to thy service, for Christ's sake. Amen.

Give us grateful hearts, our Father, for all thy mercies, and make us mindful of the needs of others; through Jesus Christ our Lord. Amen.

Lord, help us to receive all good things from thy hand and use them to thy praise. Amen.

Heavenly Father, make us thankful to thee, and mindful of others, as we receive these blessings; in Jesus' Name. Amen.

Father in heaven, sustain our bodies with this food, our hearts with true friendship, and our souls with thy truth; for Christ's sake. Amen.

O Lord God, heavenly Father, bless unto us these thy gifts which of thy tender kindness thou hast bestowed upon us; through Jesus Christ our Lord. Amen.

Master of Life, make our table-companionship a revelation of thy presence, and turn our daily bread into the bread of life. Amen.

VII.

For all Sorts and Conditions of Men

OF GENERAL INTERCESSION

O God, the Creator and Preserver of all mankind: We humbly beseech thee for all sorts and conditions of men; that thou wouldest be pleased to make thy ways known unto them, thy saving health unto all nations. More especially we pray for thy holy Church universal; that it may be so guided and governed by thy good Spirit, that all who profess and call themselves Christians may be led into the way of truth, and hold the faith in unity of spirit, in the bond of peace, and in righteousness of life. Finally, we commend to thy fatherly goodness all those who are any ways afflicted or distressed, in mind, body, or estate; that it may please thee to comfort and relieve them, according to their several necessities; giving them patience under their sufferings, and a happy issue out of all their afflictions. And this we beg for Jesus Christ's sake. Amen.

The Book of Prayers

FOR MANKIND

Eternal Father, throned in suns and stars yet near to the lowly and the contrite, hear us now as we pray, not for ourselves, but for our neighbors.

Lord of the whole earth, who hast made all nations and races of one blood, one in sin and need of pardon, one in joy and sorrow, bring us now into one obedience to thy will. Yea, set our prayers against the pride of men, and bring them to pass. Govern thou our land and guide our leaders that we may be saved from low appeal to passion and fear and be dedicate to that Spirit given through thy Son.

Lord of our common life, whose purpose is to fashion mankind into one family, cleanse thou our toil and our pleasures; and walk thou through hospital and school, through shop and office and store, through field and all the journeyings of men, that whether we work or play, it shall be for a sign to thee.

Lord of the secret soul, who knowest our infirmities before we ask and our blindness in the asking, we pray for all needy ones. Come like dawn upon all sadness, as a cool hand upon our fevered sickness, as springs of water in the desert of despair; and be pleased, we pray thee, to hold our loved ones in thy care.

Lord of the Church, who hast chosen the Church as the body of Christ, grant that the body may not war against the spirit or be weakly conformed to the fashion of the transient time. Give to the Church the piercing word of truth and a deeper love, yes, the willingness to lay down life that thy Word may be known.

God of all good life, before whom angels veil their faces, forgive the blundering of our prayers. Wherein they are true, help us to answer them, and to trust thee for answer beyond our best dream; through Jesus Christ. Amen.

FOR THE BLIND AND DEAF AND DUMB

Almighty God, in whose holy Word there is promise of a day when the eyes of the blind shall be opened, the ears of the deaf shall be unstopped, and the tongue of the dumb shall sing; of thy mercy we beseech thee for all who now live in darkness or in silence. Fortify them to bear their affliction with unwavering faith; grant to them that inner sight and hearing-ear to which thy love and beauty are ever revealed; and may they know thee as their constant friend and guide; for Jesus' sake. Amen.

FOR THE HOMELESS AND THE HUNGRY

O God, heavenly Father, I pray thee to succor all those who have nowhere to go; no bed, no comfort, and no food. Stir us all to do for them what we profess to be willing to do for thy sake, and give them a speedy relief; through Jesus Christ our Lord. Amen.

FOR THE LONELY

O Lord, thou lover of souls, in whose hand is the life of every living thing: We bring before thee in our prayers all those who are lonely in the world. Thine they are, and no one can pluck them out of thy hand. In thy pitiful mercy let our remembrance reach them and comfort their hearts, for thy love's sake. Amen.

FOR THE MISJUDGED

O Lord, strengthen and support, we entreat thee, all persons unjustly accused or underrated. Comfort them by the ever-present thought that thou knowest the whole truth, and wilt, in thine own good time, make it as clear as the light. Give them grace to pray for such as do them wrong, and hear and bless them when they pray; for the sake of Jesus Christ, our Lord and Saviour. Amen.

FOR THE SLEEPLESS

Watch thou, dear Lord, with those who wake, or watch, or weep tonight, and give thine angels charge over those who sleep. Tend thy sick ones, O Lord Christ. Rest thy weary ones. Bless thy dying ones. Pity thine afflicted ones. Shield thy joyous ones. And all, for thy love's sake. Amen.

For All Sorts and Conditions of Men

FOR THOSE WHO HAVE NONE TO PRAY FOR THEM

Accept my prayers, dear Father, for those who have no one to love them enough to pray for them. Wherever and whoever they are, give them a share of my blessings, and in thy love let them know that they are not forgotten; for Jesus' sake. Amen.

FOR ALL WHO HAVE GIVEN UP PRAYING

Forgive and bless, O Lord, those who have given up coming to thee in prayer. In thy mercy look upon them and draw them to thee, that they may feel their need and seek thee once again; for Jesus' sake. Amen.

FOR THE GODLESS

O thou who hast given us the faith of Christ for a light unto our feet amid the darkness of this world, have pity upon all who, doubting or denying it, have gone astray from the path of safety. Bring home the truth to their hearts and give them grace to receive it as little children; through Jesus Christ our Lord. Amen.

FOR TRAVELLERS

Most merciful Father, we beseech thee to protect and prosper thy servant on *his* journey. May the angel of thy presence be with *him* wherever *he* may go, and may all *his* steps be ordered of thee in wisdom and love, so that *he* shall travel with thee as *his* guardian and *his* guide, and arrive in safety at *his* desired haven. O Lord, bless *his* going out and *his* coming in, from this time forth and even for evermore; through Jesus Christ our Lord. Amen.

O Lord, we beseech thee, watch over and protect those who travel by land, or sea, or air. In the night, as in the day, let thy right hand hold them. Empower and keep steadfast all to whose skill and fidelity they have entrusted their lives, and of thy loving kindness grant them a safe journey, that with grateful hearts they may praise and serve thee; through Jesus Christ our Lord. Amen.

FOR FRIENDS IN DISTANT PLACES

O Lord our God, who art in every place, and from whom no space or distance can ever part us: Take into thy holy keeping our friends and loved ones in distant places, and grant that both they and we, by drawing near to thee, may be drawn nearer to one another; in Jesus Christ our Lord. Amen.

VIII.

Of the Armed Forces

FOR OUR COUNTRY

Be gracious unto us, O Lord, and bless us. Stretch forth the right hand of thy protection to guard our country, that we, being devoted to our nation's service, may ever be defended by thy power; through Jesus Christ our Lord. Amen.

FOR PEACE IN OUR COUNTRY

Grant us peace, O thou eternal source of peace. Bless our country, that we may ever be a stronghold of peace and the advocate of peace in the councils of nations. May contentment reign within our borders, health and happiness within our homes. Strengthen the bonds of friendship and fellowship among all the inhabitants of our land. Inspire virtue in every soul; and may the love of thy Name hallow every home and every heart. Praised be thou, O Lord, Giver of Peace. Amen.

O God, who wouldest fold both heaven and earth in a single peace: Let the design of thy great love lighten upon the waste of our wraths and sorrows; and give peace to thy Church, peace among nations, peace in our dwellings, and peace in our hearts; through thy Son our Saviour Jesus Christ. Amen.

FOR THOSE IN THE ARMED FORCES

O Lord God, our Father, our Saviour, our might, we commend to thy keeping all those who are venturing their lives on our behalf: That whether by life or by death they may win for the whole world the fruits of their sacrifice, and a holy peace; through Jesus Christ our Lord. Amen.

O Lord God of hosts, stretch forth, we pray thee, thine almighty arm to strengthen the men and women of our armed forces. Keep them temperate in all things, that they may serve thee without stumbling and without stain. For their homes, give them steadfast loyalty through all the days of separation; for their church, give them reverence and devotion; and grant that, returning with greater insight into thy purpose, they may lead us into greater service in thy kingdom; through Jesus Christ our Lord. Amen.

FOR COURAGE IN COMBAT

O God, make me ready to face what I must, prepared, trained, unafraid, willing, in the faith that if I do my utmost, my effort will not be lost. For Jesus' sake. Amen.

Of the Armed Forces

O God, with whom nothing shall be impossible: Grant me that courage which comes only from perfect union with thee, the infinite source of all power and might, so that I may meet whatever thou dost send me with serenity and peace, and never fail to think brave thoughts, to speak brave words, and to do brave deeds. I ask this in the Name of him who died for me, my Saviour Jesus Christ. Amen.

Be thou unto us, O Lord, a tower of strength, a place of refuge, and a defense against the enemy. Let thy comfort support and strengthen us, thy mercy keep us, and thy grace guide us. Amen.

O God, who art the author of peace and lover of concord, in knowledge of whom standeth our eternal life, whose service is perfect freedom: Defend us thy humble servants in all assaults of our enemies; that we, surely trusting in thy defense, may not fear the power of any adversaries; through the might of Jesus Christ our Lord. Amen.

FOR LOYAL SERVICE

Dear Father in heaven, I, thy child, come to thee and ask thy divine protection and gracious guidance while I am serving my country. By the precious blood of thy Son thou hast bought me as thine own. Thou hast assured me that the very hairs of my head are all numbered. Trusting in thy promise and relying on thy grace, I confidently ask thee to guard me against all danger and deliver me from all evil of body and soul. Yet it is thy will and not my own that I would serve.

O Jesus, my Redeemer, let me never forget what it cost thee to redeem me, so that the memory of thy bitter suffering and death may keep me from sin and wickedness. Wash me daily in thy blood. Cleanse me from all my transgressions and iniquities and by thy grace enable me to follow in thy footsteps, so that thou never needest be ashamed of me.

O Holy Ghost, strengthen me in the hour of temptation. Keep me pure in heart and chaste in body, obedient to my superiors, considerate to all my fellow soldiers, a living example of true Christian faith.

O thou God of my salvation, let me be and remain thine own in time and eternity. Amen.

FOR THE WOUNDED

Have mercy, O Lord, upon the wounded and the suffering, whether of our own people or of the enemy. Let thy grace be their comfort, although natural friends be far away. Raise them to health, if it be good, but chiefly give them such faith and patience that they may glorify thee upon the earth; through Jesus Christ our Lord. Amen.

Of the Armed Forces

Thou Father of all men, revealed in him who hast commanded us not to return evil for evil but to pray for those who hate us: Enable us by his blessed example and his loving Spirit to pray sincerely for our enemies. When we have offended, forgive us and help us to find a way of reconciliation. Let not anger burn between us but deliver them and us from the power of hatred, that we may be as ready to grant forgiveness as to ask it, and grant that thy peace may rule in all our hearts, both now and evermore. Amen.

IX.

Of National Life

THANKSGIVING FOR MANY BLESSINGS

Most gracious God, we give thee hearty thanks for this good land in which our heritage is cast, for freedom to worship thee, for the glory of a people set at liberty, for the government in which we share. Keep us ever mindful of the responsibilities thereby laid upon us and faithful to our trust; through him who is the truth that alone can make men free, even thy Son Jesus Christ our Lord. Amen.

O God, who by thy providence didst lead our forefathers to this land wherein they found refuge from oppression and freedom to worship thee: We beseech thee ever to guide our nation in the way of thy truth and peace, so that we may never fail in the blessing which thou hast promised to that people whose God is the Lord; through Jesus Christ thy Son our Lord. Amen.

FOR NATIONAL PURITY

Lord God Almighty, defend our land, we beseech thee, from the secret power and the open shame of great national sins. From all dishonesty and civic corruption, from all vainglory and selfish luxury, from all cruelty and the spirit of violence, from covetousness which is idolatry, from impurity which defiles the temple of the Holy Spirit, and from intemperance which is the mother of many crimes and sorrows, good Lord, deliver and save us, and our children, and our children's children, in the land which thou hast blessed with the light of pure religion; through Jesus Christ, our only Saviour and King. Amen.

IN A NATIONAL CRISIS

King of kings and Lord of lords, thou Lord of life and death, protect our nation in its great need. Let men use this trial to turn to thee for strength and to find in Jesus their peace with thee. Let wise counsel, calm thinking, unselfish aims prevail. Grant unity to the land and support of all just measures. In Jesus' Name. Amen.

FOR THE PRESIDENT AND OTHERS IN AUTHORITY

O Lord, our Governor, whose glory is in all the world: We commend this nation to thy merciful care that, being guided by thy providence, we may dwell secure in thy peace. Grant to the President of the United States, and to all in authority, wisdom and strength to know and to do thy will. Fill them with the love of truth and righteousness, and make them ever mindful of their calling to serve this people in thy fear;

The Book of Prayers

through Jesus Christ our Lord, who liveth and reigneth with thee and the Holy Ghost, one God, world without end. Amen.

FOR CONGRESS

Most gracious God, we humbly beseech thee, as for the people of these United States in general, so especially for their senate and representatives in congress assembled, that thou wouldest be pleased to direct and prosper all their consultations, to the advancement of thy glory, the good of thy Church, the safety, honor, and welfare of thy people; that all things may be so ordered and settled by their endeavors, upon the best and surest foundations, that peace and happiness, truth and justice, religion and piety, may be established among us for all generations. These and all other necessities for them, for us, and thy whole Church, we humbly beg in the name and mediation of Jesus Christ, our most blessed Lord and Saviour. Amen.

FOR COURTS OF JUSTICE

Almighty God, who sittest in the throne judging right: We humbly beseech thee to bless the courts of justice and the magistrates in all this land, and give unto them the spirit of wisdom and understanding, that they may discern the truth, and impartially administer the law in the fear of thee alone; through him who shall come to be our judge, thy Son our Saviour Jesus Christ. Amen.

Of National Life

FOR GOOD LEADERS

O Lord, open the eyes of those who govern this nation that they may see thy purpose, and grant them obedience speedily to fulfil it; through Jesus Christ our Lord. Amen.

OF NEW AMERICANS

Our Father, we thank thee for the men and women of every race and nation, class and creed, who have given their best in thought and work for the building of our country. Grant that we may continue always to live in harmony together and to benefit from the richness and variety of all contributions to our national greatness. Keep us humble and tolerant and willing to learn from one another. Make us obedient to thee, the one God and Father of us all, and by our talents and service, dedicated to thee and our fellow citizens, preserve our nation in united strength under thee; through Jesus Christ our Lord. Amen.

FOR INDUSTRIAL HARMONY

O God, who hast taught us that we are members one of another: Remove, we beseech thee, from among us all distrust and bitterness in industrial disputes; and grant that, seeking what is just and equal, and caring for the needs of others, we may live and work together in unity and love; through Jesus Christ our Lord. Amen.

O God, the Father of all mankind: We beseech thee to inspire our citizens with such love, truth, and equity, that in all our dealings one with another we may show forth our brotherhood in thee; for the sake of Jesus Christ our Lord. Amen.

FOR THE RIGHT USE OF SCIENCE

Deliver us, O Lord, from abuse of our sciences and skills, lest we become a people perished for want of knowledge. Teach us so to use our learning that it may fulfil and not destroy the precious fabric of our peaceful life, that we die not as fools for want of wisdom. Amen.

FOR OUR NATION'S SCHOOLS

O Lord, we pray thee to bless and prosper the cause of education. Bless the boys and girls who are in school and the young men and women in colleges and universities. Guide them into the knowledge of thy truth and teach them to do thy will. Bless all teachers and enrich their lives with the knowledge of Christ. Bless the colleges and educational institutions that they may be centers of sound learning and true light; in the Name of the great teacher, Jesus Christ. Amen.

FOR TEACHERS

Bless, O Lord, all who teach: Grant to them a patient and loving understanding and give them the joy of seeing the fruits of their labors in happy lives. Amen.

Of National Life

O Lord, look down in mercy upon our country at this time and bless all those who by virtue of their citizenship are called to make choice of fit persons to serve in the councils of this nation, that all things may be established among us with peace and justice. Give honesty, truthfulness, strength, and wisdom to those who govern, and grant us grace and willingness to do our part in supporting their great work for thee; through Jesus Christ our Lord. Amen.

X.

For God's Gifts and Graces

FOR CALMNESS

O God, who art a hiding place from the wind and a shelter from the storm, help us to turn from the tumult and clamor of the world to the calm of thy great assurance; through Jesus Christ our Lord. Amen.

FOR CHRISTLIKENESS

O Lord our Christ, may we have thy mind and thy Spirit. Make us instruments of thy peace. Where there is hatred, let us sow love; where there is injury, pardon; where there is discord, union; where there is doubt, faith; where there is despair, hope; where there is darkness, light; and where there is sadness, joy.

O divine Master, grant that we may not so much seek to be consoled as to console; to be understood, as to understand; to be loved, as to love; for it is in giving that we receive; it is in pardoning that we are pardoned; and it is in dying that we are born to eternal life. Amen.

For God's Gifts and Graces

FOR COURAGE

God, I do not ask for courage for the whole of life but rather for courage to live a moment at a time, and that moment for thee. Amen.

FOR GENEROSITY

Lord, we pray thee to give us grace to be generous toward others and stern with ourselves, that so we may enter into fulness of life and glorify thee amongst men; through Jesus Christ our Lord. Amen.

FOR FAITH

O God of hope, fill us, we beseech thee, with all joy and peace in believing, that we may ever abound in hope by the power of thy Holy Spirit, and show forth our thankfulness to thee in trustful and courageous lives; through Jesus Christ our Lord and Saviour. Amen.

FOR CHRISTIAN GLADNESS

O God, author of the world's joy, bearer of the world's pain: Make us glad that we are men and that we have inherited the world's burden; deliver us from the luxury of cheap melancholy; and, at the heart of all our trouble and sorrow, let unconquerable gladness dwell; through our Lord and Saviour Jesus Christ. Amen.

The Book of Prayers

FOR THE GOOD USE OF LIFE

Eternal God, who committest to us the swift and solemn trust of life; since we know not what a day may bring forth, but only that the hour for serving thee is always present, may we wake to the instant claims of thy holy will; not waiting for tomorrow, but yielding today. Lay to rest, by the persuasion of thy spirit, the resistance of our passion, indolence, or fear. Consecrate with thy presence the way our feet may go, and the humblest work will shine, and the roughest place be made plain. Lift us above unrighteous anger and mistrust into faith, and hope, and charity, by a simple and steadfast reliance on thy sure will; and so may we be modest in our time of wealth, patient under disappointment, ready for danger, serene in death. In all things draw us to the mind of Christ, that thy lost image may be traced again, and thou mayest own us at one with him and thee. Amen.

FOR GROWTH IN GRACE

O Lord our God, grant us grace to desire thee with our whole heart, that so desiring we may seek and find thee, and so finding thee may love thee, and loving thee may hate those sins from which thou hast redeemed us. Amen.

For God's Gifts and Graces

FOR GUIDANCE

O heavenly Father, in whom we live and move and have our being: We humbly pray thee so to guide and govern us by thy Holy Spirit that, in all the cares and occupations of our daily life, we may never forget thee, but remember that we are ever walking in thy sight; through Jesus Christ our Lord. Amen.

FOR HUMILITY

Take from us, O Lord, all pride and vanity, all boasting and forwardness, and give us the true courage that shows itself by gentleness, the true wisdom that shows itself by simplicity, and the true power that shows itself by humility; through Jesus Christ our Lord. Amen.

FOR INSPIRATION

Lord, take my lips, and speak through them; take my mind, and think through it; take my heart, and set it on fire. Amen.

FOR JOY IN GOD'S CREATION

O heavenly Father, who hast filled the world with beauty: Open our eyes, we beseech thee, to behold thy gracious hand in all thy works; that rejoicing in thy whole creation, we may learn to serve thee with gladness; for the sake of him by whom all things were made, thy Son Jesus Christ our Lord. Amen.

The Book of Prayers

FOR KNOWLEDGE OF GOD

O thou who art the light of the minds that know thee, the life of the souls that love thee, and the strength of the thoughts that seek thee: Help us so to know thee that we may truly love thee, so to love thee that we may fully serve thee, whose service is perfect freedom; through Jesus Christ our Lord. Amen.

FOR LOVE OF GOD

O faithful Lord, grant us, I pray thee, faithful hearts devoted to thee, and to the service of all men for thy sake. Fill us with pure love of thee, keep us steadfast in this love, give us faith that worketh by love, and preserve us faithful unto death. Amen.

O God, the God of all goodness and grace, who art worthy of a greater love than we can either give or understand: Fill our hearts, we beseech thee, with such love toward thee as may cast out all sloth and fear, that nothing may seem too hard for us to do or suffer in obedience to thee; and grant that by thus loving, we may become daily more like unto thee, and finally obtain the crown of life which thou hast promised to those who unfeignedly love thee; through Jesus Christ our Lord. Amen.

For God's Gifts and Graces

FOR LOYALTY

Teach us, good Lord, to serve thee as thou deservest; to give and not to count the cost; to fight and not to heed the wounds; to toil and not to seek for rest; to labor and not to ask for any reward, save that of knowing that we do thy will; through Jesus Christ our Lord. Amen.

FOR PATIENCE

O God, give me the serenity to accept what cannot be changed——

Give me the courage to change what can be changed——

The wisdom to know one from the other. Amen.

FOR A PROPER APPROACH TO PRAYER

O almighty God, from whom every good prayer cometh, and who pourest out on all who desire it the spirit of grace and supplications: Deliver us, when we draw nigh to thee, from coldness of heart and wanderings of mind, that with steadfast thoughts and kindled affections we may worship thee in spirit and in truth; through Jesus Christ our Lord. Amen.

FOR THE PRESENCE OF GOD

O living Christ, make us conscious of thy healing nearness. Touch our eyes that we may see thee, open our ears that we may hear thy voice, enter our hearts that we may know thy love. Overshadow our souls and bodies with thy presence that we may partake of thy strength, thy love, and thy healing life. Amen.

O God, who art, and wast, and art to come; before whose face the generations rise and pass away: Age after age the living seek thee and find that of thy faithfulness there is no end. Our fathers in their pilgrimage walked by thy guidance, and rested on thy compassion; still to their children be thou the cloud by day and the fire by night. Where but in thee have we a covert from the storm or a shadow from the heat of life? In our manifold temptations thou alone knowest and art ever nigh; in sorrow, thy pity revives the fainting soul; in our prosperity and ease, it is thy Spirit only that can keep us from our pride and keep us humble. O thou only source of peace and righteousness, take now the veil from every heart, and join us in one communion with thy prophets and saints, who have trusted in thee and were not ashamed. Not of our worthiness, but of thy tender mercy, hear our prayer; for the sake of Jesus Christ thy Son our Lord. Amen.

Lord, keep me ever near to thee. Let nothing separate me from thee, let nothing keep me back from thee. If I fall, bring me back quickly to thee, and make me hope in thee, trust in thee, love thee everlastingly. Amen.

For God's Gifts and Graces

FOR GOD'S PROTECTION

O almighty and most merciful God, of thy bountiful goodness keep us, we beseech thee, from all things that may hurt us, that we, being ready both in body and soul, may cheerfully accomplish those things which thou commandest; through Jesus Christ thy Son our Lord, who liveth and reigneth with thee and the Holy Ghost, ever one God, world without end. Amen.

O most loving Father, in darkness and in light, in sorrow and in joy, in life and in death, may we feel thy hand laid upon us, and abide in the peace of thy children, now and evermore; through Jesus Christ our Lord and Saviour. Amen.

FOR PURITY

Almighty God, unto whom all hearts are open, all desires known, and from whom no secrets are hid: Cleanse the thoughts of our hearts by the inspiration of thy Holy Spirit that we may perfectly love thee and worthily magnify thy Holy Name; through Jesus Christ our Lord. Amen.

FOR GREATER SPIRITUALITY

Behold, Lord, an empty vessel that needs to be filled. My Lord, fill it. I am weak in the faith; strengthen thou me. I am cold in love; warm me and make me fervent that my love may go out to my neighbor. I do not have a strong and firm faith; at times I doubt and am unable to trust thee altogether. O Lord, help me. Strengthen my faith and trust in thee. In thee I have sealed the treasures of all I have. I am poor; thou art rich and didst come to be merciful to the poor. I am a sinner; thou art upright. With me there is an abundance of sin; in thee is the fullness of righteousness. Therefore, I will remain with thee of whom I can receive but to whom I may not give. Amen.

FOR TRUST IN GOD

O Lord God, in whom we live and move and have our being, open our eyes that we may behold thy fatherly presence ever about us. Draw our hearts to thee with the power of thy love. Teach us to be anxious for nothing, and when we have done what thou hast given us to do, help us, O God our Saviour, to leave the issue to thy wisdom. Take from us all doubt and mistrust. Lift our thoughts up to thee in heaven, and make us to know that all things are possible to us through thy Son our Redeemer. Amen.

FOR CHRISTIAN VIRTUE

Hear our prayers, O Lord, and consider our desires. Give unto us true humility, a meek and quiet spirit, a loving, friendly, holy, and useful manner of life, bearing the burdens of our neighbors, denying ourselves, and studying to benefit others and to please thee in all things. Grant us to be righteous in performing promises, loving to our relatives, careful of our charges, gentle and easy to be entreated, slow to anger, and readily prepared for every good work. Amen.

FOR THE DESIRE TO WORSHIP

Eternal God, who hast formed all hearts to love thee and created all desires to be unsatisfied save in thee, quicken within our souls a continuing longing to worship thee. Wherever we may be, enable us to draw near to thee in spirit and in truth. In quietness and confidence we would open the door that thou mayest enter. Do for us what we cannot do for ourselves.

We bring to thee our consciences, dulled and insensitive. Quicken them by thy holiness. We bring to thee our minds, captured by the trivial and partial. Feed them with thy truth. We lift before thee our imaginations, stained by impurity. Purge them by thy beauty. We lift our hearts, wherein selfishness dwells. Open them to thy love. Into thy hands we place our wayward wills. Fashion them to thy purpose.

Send us from our worship into the affairs of life so strengthened within by thy Spirit that we may be co-workers with thee, revealed in Jesus Christ our Lord. Amen.

XI.

Of Godly Living

OF THANKSGIVING

O God, our heavenly Father, from whom cometh down every perfect gift: We thank and praise thy Name for all thy mercies, and for every blessing we have received from thee; for health and strength, for food and raiment, for our homes, our parents, our children, and our friends; for the work thou hast given us to do, and the strength thou hast given us to do it; for comfort in sorrow, for deliverance from danger; and if there be any special mercies not present to our minds we thank thee for them. Most of all, with thy Church throughout the world, we bless thee for thy love and compassion manifested toward us in Jesus Christ our Saviour: that through him a new and living way hath been opened up to thee, and that by his Gospel life and immortality have been brought to light. Thanks be unto thee, O God, for thine unspeakable gift; and grant that we may be so filled with a sense of thy love that as we have freely received from thee, we may freely give unto others, and may glorify thee with our bodies and spirits which are thine, which thou hast redeemed, and which thou preservest from day to day; through Jesus Christ our Lord. Amen.

Glory be to thee, O God, for all thy goodness to us and to all men: For the world in which thou hast placed us, with all its wonder and beauty, for life and health, for food and clothing, for friends and homes, for thy care that guards us always, and thy faithfulness that never fails; most of all for Jesus Christ, thine only Son our Saviour, who came into this world and died for us upon the Cross, and who hath revealed to us the love that passeth knowledge. We praise thee, O God, Father, Son, and Holy Spirit, world without end. Amen.

OF REPENTANCE

Eternal God, in whom we live and move and have our being, whose face is hidden from us by our sins, and whose mercy we forget in the blindness of our hearts: Cleanse us, we beseech thee, from all our offenses, and deliver us from proud thoughts and vain desires, that with lowliness and meekness we may draw near to thee, confessing our faults, confiding in thy grace, and finding in thee our refuge and our strength; through Jesus Christ thy Son. Amen.

Almighty God, have mercy upon us, forgive us all our sins, and deliver us from all evil; confirm and strengthen us in all goodness, and bring us to life ever-lasting; through Jesus Christ our Lord. Amen.

Almighty and most merciful Father: We have erred, and strayed from thy ways, like lost sheep. We have followed too much the devices and desires of our own hearts. We have offended against thy holy laws. We have left undone those things which we ought to have done; and we have done those things which we ought not to have done; and there is no health in us. But thou, O Lord, have mercy upon us, miserable offenders. Spare thou those, O God, who confess their faults. Restore thou those who are penitent; according to thy promises declared unto mankind in Christ Jesus our Lord. And grant, O most merciful Father, for his sake, that we may hereafter live a godly, righteous, and sober life, to the glory of thy holy Name. Amen.

IN PRAISE OF GOD

Great art thou, O Lord, and greatly to be praised; great is thy power, and thy wisdom is infinite. Thee would we praise without ceasing. Thou callest us to delight in thy praise, for thou hast made us for thyself, and our hearts find no rest until we rest in thee; to whom with the Father and the Holy Ghost all glory, praise, and honor be ascribed, both now and for ever-more. Amen.

Of Godly Living

O most high, almighty, good Lord God, to thee belong praise, glory, honor, and all blessing!

Praised be my Lord God with all his creatures, and especially our brother the sun, who bringeth us the day and who bringeth us the light; fair is he and shineth with a very great splendor: O Lord, he signifieth to us thee!

Praised be my Lord for our sister the moon, and for the stars, the which he hath set clear and lovely in heaven.

Praised be my Lord for our brother the wind, and for air and cloud, calms and all weather by the which thou upholdest life in all creatures.

Praised be my Lord for our sister water, who is very serviceable unto us and humble and precious and clean.

Praised be my Lord for our brother fire, through whom thou givest us light in the darkness; and he is bright and pleasant and very mighty and strong.

Praised be my Lord for our mother the earth, the which doth sustain us and keep us, and bringeth forth divers fruits and flowers of many colors, and grass.

Praised be my Lord for all those who pardon one another for his love's sake, and who endure weakness and tribulation; blessed are they who peaceably shall endure, for thou, O most Highest, shalt give them a crown.

Praised be my Lord for our sister, the death of the body, from which no man escapeth. Woe to him who dieth in mortal sin! Blessed are they who are found walking by thy most holy will, for the second death shall have no power to do them harm.

Praise ye and bless the Lord, and give thanks unto him and serve him with great humility. Amen.

ON ENTERING CHURCH

O God, thou source of all pure desires and holy affections: Give me now a quiet mind and a reverent and devout heart that I may worthily worship thee at this time. Amen.

O God our Father, may the meditations of our hearts, in this hour, be acceptable in thy sight; may we strive for a new understanding of thy Word and will; may we here resolve upon a more complete obedience to thy commands, a richer ministry to thy people and purpose. Through thy Spirit lift us up into a greater steadfastness, a finer courage, a fuller loyalty, a devotion worthy of those who name themselves after thee; through Jesus Christ our Lord. Amen.

ON LEAVING CHURCH

Grant, O Lord, that what hath been said with our lips we may believe in our hearts, and that what we believe in our hearts we may practice in our lives; through Jesus Christ our Lord. Amen.

Of Godly Living

Almighty God, who hast come into our valley of earth in Jesus Christ, his life is an open way for us into the holiest of all, his death is thy love bearing and bearing away our sins, his resurrection is pledge of eternal life to all who believe, his Spirit is thy present gift to all who would pray in sincerity and truth. Thanks be to thee for so great a salvation! Now give us grace to wait for thee, and to watch for thee, and to wish for thee, until the breaking of the day; through the same Jesus Christ our Lord. Amen.

BEFORE COMMUNION

Cleanse the thoughts of our hearts, O Lord, as we come to partake of thy holy sacrament, and enlighten our minds by thy Holy Spirit, that we may be delivered from all insincerity, from satisfaction with ourselves, and from failure to see how great is our need of thy grace. This we ask for thy Name's sake. Amen.

AFTER COMMUNION

Grant, O Lord, that the ears which have heard the voice of thy songs may be closed to the voice of clamor and dispute, that the eyes which have seen thy great love may also behold thy blessed hope, that the tongues which have sung thy praise may speak the truth, that the feet which have walked in thy courts may walk in the region of light, and that the souls of all who have received thy blessed sacrament may be restored to newness of life. Glory be to thee for thine unspeakable gift. Amen.

O God, who hast so greatly loved us, long sought us, and mercifully redeemed us: Give us grace that in everything we may yield ourselves, our wills, and our works, a continual thank offering unto thee; through Jesus Christ our Lord. Amen.

ON JOINING THE CHURCH

Strengthen, O Lord, by thy Holy Spirit, thy servant who is now about to take the vows of membership in the Church. Grant that he may confess thee boldly before men and grow in the grace and knowledge of our Lord and Saviour Jesus Christ and be found worthy to be numbered among thy people; through the same Jesus Christ our Lord. Amen.

XII.

In the Twilight of Life

OF THANKSGIVING FOR THE GIFT OF LIFE

O Lord, from whom I have received so much, grant unto me this blessing—make my heart grateful for the gift of life. In Christ's Name. Amen.

OF GRATITUDE FOR A LONG LIFE

O God, I thank thee for the many years of my life. As I grow older I am conscious how quickly time flies; therefore grant me the desire to apply my heart unto heavenly wisdom, that my remaining days may be spent to thy glory; through Jesus Christ our Lord. Amen.

OF THANKSGIVING FOR GRANDCHILDREN

Thou hast given me the privilege of seeing my children's children, and I thank thee; may the brightness of their youth be an added light to my years; and may I be used for their benefit; through Jesus Christ our Lord. Amen.

OF BLESSING ON GROWNUP CHILDREN

Bless, O Lord, my children, now grown up and no longer under my care; give them health and strength to play a worthy part in life; may they still be influenced by the lessons learned at home; and unite us all at last in the home which is above; through Jesus Christ our Lord. Amen.

FOR A CHEERFUL SPIRIT

O Lord, give me a cheerful spirit, that in spite of age or infirmity I may be a help to others; may thankfulness take the place of grumbling and trust the place of worry that I may grow in serenity of character; through Jesus Christ our Lord. Amen.

FOR GOOD HEALTH

Grant unto me, O Lord, good health according to the years of my life; give me clarity of mind, freedom from anxiety, and a restful spirit, that stayed upon thee I may grow in understanding of thy perfect peace; through the merits of Jesus Christ our Lord. Amen.

FOR THE NEARNESS OF GOD

Lord, thou hast been our dwelling place in all generations. Before the mountains were brought forth or ever thou hadst formed the earth and the world, even from everlasting to everlasting, thou art God. Thou turnest man to destruction and sayest, Return, ye children of men. For a thousand years in thy sight are but as yesterday when it is past, and as a watch in the night.

In the Twilight of Life

Thou who art Lord of time and eternity, let me live daily in thy presence, and when thou callest me, take me evermore to dwell with thee. Amen.

FOR HARMONY WITH GOD'S WILL

O God, who art our refuge and our strength and as the shadow of a great rock in a weary land, help me living and dying to yield myself to thee in faith and love. All along life's journey thou hast led me when I would reach out to touch thy hand; thou wilt not forsake me now. Go with me into the dark and on beyond to the glorious brightness of thine eternity.

For Jesus Christ our Lord, I give thee thanks above all earthly mercies. To him I pledge my loyalty and devotion to thy service, that I may be used as thou wilt for the forwarding of thy kingdom. In his Name I pray. Amen.

FOR STRENGTH TO BEAR INFIRMITIES

May this pain, and all I have to bear, remind me of the greater pains our Saviour suffered for me; and grant me an uncomplaining spirit, like Jesus my Lord. Amen.

ON FACING DEATH

O Lord, let not the uncertainty of the future dismay me, or the lurking shadows bring me to despair; but with the lamp of hope burning brightly, may I complete my long pilgrimage, and at last come to the glories of the perfect day; through Jesus Christ our Lord. Amen.

O Lord, support us all the day long, until the shadows lengthen and the evening comes, and the busy world is hushed, and the fever of life is over, and our work is done. Then in thy mercy grant us a safe lodging, and a holy rest, and peace at the last. Amen.

Abide with us now, O Lord, for it is toward evening and the day is far spent. O thou who neither slumberest nor sleepest, evermore be with thy children. As thou coverest the earth with darkness, cover us with thine infinite mercy; through Jesus Christ our Lord. Amen.

XIII.

For Those Who Are Sick

FOR THE SUFFERING

O Lord, who dost feel the pain of the world: Look down upon all sick and suffering persons; enfold them with thy love, that in the midst of pain they may find thy presence; to doctors and nurses grant tender hearts and healing hands; and, if it be thy will, give health again; for thy tender mercy's sake. Amen.

O Lord, look down from heaven, behold, visit, and relieve this thy servant. Look upon *him* with the eyes of thy mercy, give *him* comfort and sure confidence in thee, defend *him* in all danger, and keep *him* in perpetual peace and safety; through Jesus Christ our Lord. Amen.

O God, the strength of the weak and the comfort of sufferers: Mercifully accept our prayers, and grant to thy servant the help of thy power, that, according to thy good pleasure, *his* sickness may be turned into health, and our sorrow into joy; through Jesus Christ our Lord. Amen.

FOR A SICK CHILD

O heavenly Father, watch with us, we pray thee, over the sick child for whom our prayers are offered, and grant that *he* may be restored to that perfect health which it is thine alone to give; through Jesus Christ our Lord. Amen.

FOR THOSE IN MENTAL DARKNESS

O heavenly Father, we beseech thee to have mercy upon all thy children who are living in mental darkness. Restore them, if it pleaseth thee, to strength of mind and cheerfulness of spirit, and give them health and peace; through Jesus Christ our Lord. Amen.

FOR AN ALCOHOLIC

Gracious God, the helper of all who put their trust in thee, we pray for those who are enslaved by intoxicants, especially for —— Give *him*, O Lord, the desire and the will to be free, and the grace to continue in the right way; and show us how to help *him* and to lead *him* to thee who art our hope and strength. Amen.

FOR A PERSON UNDERGOING SURGERY

Bless thy servant, O Lord God, and grant to *him* the trust and relaxation that is needful. Give the sur-

For Those Who Are Sick

geons and nurses thy grace, that by their ministrations thy will may be accomplished in loving service. Amen.

THANKSGIVING FOR THE RECOVERY
OF A SICK PERSON

O Lord, whose compassions fail not and whose mercies are new every morning: We give thee hearty thanks that it hath pleased thee to give to this our *brother* both relief from pain and hope of renewed health. Continue, we beseech thee, in *him* the good work that thou hast begun, that, daily increasing in bodily strength, *he* may so order *his* life as always to think and do such things as shall please thee: through Jesus Christ our Lord. Amen.

FOR THE DYING

Into thy hands, O Lord, we commend the spirit of our loved one, now passing from us into thy eternal presence. Lord Jesus receive *him* into thy holy keeping. In the name of the Father and of the Son and of the Holy Ghost. Amen.

XIV.
In Time of Sickness

O God, the Father of lights, from whom cometh down every good and perfect gift: Mercifully look upon our frailty and infirmity and grant us such health of body as thou knowest to be needful for us; that, both in our bodies and souls, we may evermore serve thee with all our strength and might; through Jesus Christ our Lord. Amen.

Almighty God, who didst send thy son Jesus Christ to be the great physician of our souls and bodies: Grant us thy peace. Thou who givest rest to those who wait upon thee, grant us thy courage. In quietness and confidence may we find strength. Give wisdom and skill to the doctors and nurses. We give ourselves into thy sustaining presence, knowing that in thee is our peace; through Jesus Christ our Lord. Amen.

ON PAIN

We ask thee not, O Lord, to rid us of pain; but grant in thy mercy that our pain may be free from waste, unfretted by rebellion against thy will, un-

In Time of Sickness

soiled by thought of ourselves, purified by love of our kind, and ennobled by devotion to thy kingdom; through the merits of thine only Son our Lord. Amen.

FOR SLEEP

Gracious Lord, who slumberest not but who dost ever keep watch over thy children: Be thou the companion to the shadows this night. As the dews of quietness settle upon the flowers of the field, so still my spirit that my body may relax into the blessedness of sleep. Unto thee I commit my faults, my errors, and my restlessness, as I rest in thine everlasting arms. In Jesus Christ's name. Amen.

BEFORE SURGERY

O loving Father, I commit myself with perfect trust into thy loving hands. Watch over me and protect me in my hour of weakness, and grant that as I become unconscious of earthly things my thoughts may be turned to thee. Bless and guide thy servants who shall tend me; and grant that I may so bear suffering with cheerful courage that I may be the means, under thy hand, of helping others in their time of trial; for Jesus Christ's sake. Amen.

AFTER SURGERY

Bless the Lord, O my soul, and all that is within me, bless his holy Name. O thou merciful Father in heaven, thou hast fulfilled thy promises and been with me in the hour of fear and pain. When I was weak and helpless, thou didst furnish me strength. I called upon thee in my trouble; thou didst deliver me, and I now glorify thee. Thou didst bless the surgeon's skill and safely bring me through the operation. My sins and weaknesses thou didst forgive for Christ's sake. O gracious Father, continue thy favors upon me, and if it be thy will, grant me full and speedy recovery. Bestow on me the boon of a restful day, and let the night come with refreshing sleep. As thou watchest over me in these trying days, grant me patience and guide my thoughts to dwell on thy goodness. Thou art my shepherd; make me confident that I shall not want. O gracious Father, I cast all my cares upon thee, for thou carest for me. Hear my prayer; for the sake of Jesus Christ, my dear Saviour. Amen.

OF THANKSGIVING FOR RECOVERY OF HEALTH

Almighty God, in whose hands are all our ways, I thank thee that in thy mercy I have come safely through my sickness and have my health again. Help me now to show my thankfulness to thee by serving thee more faithfully in my daily life and by sharing more sacrificingly in the work of thy holy Church; through Jesus Christ our Lord. Amen.

O thou loving Father, whose healing power has touched my life in its hours of pain and distress, and

In Time of Sickness

has now set it upon the road to recovery, thou hast sustained me in my weakness and supported me in my pain. As thou then hast given me energy to endure, so now, O Lord, give me patience to persist. Grant that my continuing thanksgiving may be expressed in finding thy will for my life and in following it from this day and evermore; through Jesus Christ our Lord. Amen.

DURING A LONG CONVALESCENCE

Eternal God, for whom a thousand years are but as yesterday when it is past and as a watch in the night: Speak patience to my restless spirit and hold my eagerness in check until at length restored health, if that be thy purpose, may enable me to live fully for myself, for my loved ones, for my fellow men, and for thee. In Jesus' Name. Amen.

XV.

In Time of Sorrow, Trouble, Need

FOR CALMNESS AND REST

O God of peace, who hast taught us that in returning and rest we shall be saved, in quietness and in
confidence shall be our strength: By the might of thy
Spirit lift us, we pray thee, to thy presence, where we
may be still and know that thou art God; through
Jesus Christ our Lord. Amen.

Deepen, O Lord, the stillness of our inmost thoughts,
and refresh us with the quiet springs of thine eternity; that we may know thy peace which passeth
understanding, and love thee with an everlasting love;
through Jesus Christ our Lord. Amen.

FOR COURAGE

Take my hands, O my Master, and give me strength
to overcome my fears; deepen my trust, and the fears
shall vanish away. I will lift up mine eyes to thee, and
in thy power I shall go onward in thy way. Blessed

be God who giveth us the victory. For Jesus' sake. Amen.

BEFORE AN IMPORTANT DECISION

O make thy way plain before my face. Support me this day under all the difficulties I shall meet. I offer myself to thee, O God, this day to do in me, and with me, as to thee seems most meet. Amen.

O God, by whom the meek are guided in judgment, and light riseth up in darkness for the godly: Grant us, in all our doubts and uncertainties, the grace to ask what thou wouldest have us to do, that the spirit of wisdom may save us from all false choices, and that in thy light we may see light, and in thy straight path may not stumble; through Jesus Christ our Lord. Amen.

IN DESPONDENCY

O Lord, who art as the shadow of a great rock in a weary land, who beholdest thy weak creatures, weary of labor, weary of pleasure, weary of hope deferred, weary of self: In thine abundant compassion and un-utterable tenderness, bring us, we pray thee, unto thy rest. Amen.

Thou knowest, O Lord, what most I require; help me, and out of the treasury of thy goodness, succor thou my needy soul. Amen.

[89]

FOR A QUICKENING OF FAITH

O Father and God of all comfort, grant us through thy Word and Holy Spirit a firm, happy, and grateful faith whereby we may readily overcome this and every other trial, and at length realize that it is the truth when thy dear son Jesus Christ himself says: Be of good cheer, I have overcome the world. Amen.

Grant, Lord, that I may not, for one moment, admit willingly into my soul any thought contrary to thy love. Amen.

IN TIME OF FEAR

O most loving Father, who willest us to give thanks for all things, to dread nothing but the loss of thee, and to cast all our cares on thee who carest for us: Preserve us from faithless fears and worldly anxieties, and grant that no clouds of this mortal life may hide from us the light of that love which is immortal, and which thou hast manifested to us in thy Son, Jesus Christ our Lord. Amen.

O Lord, fix my soul on thee; let me not weary myself with cares and anxieties and harassments of this life, who hopes to live with thee in thine everlasting love. Let me not be anxious about anything, save that thou shouldest love me, and make my soul as thou lovest and willest. Amen.

In Time of Sorrow, Trouble, Need

O Lord my God, be not thou far from me; my God, have regard to help me; for there have risen up against me sundry thoughts and great fears afflicting my soul. How shall I pass through unhurt? How shall I break them to pieces? This is my hope, my one only consolation, to flee unto thee in every tribulation, to trust in thee, to call upon thee from my inmost heart, and to wait patiently for thy consolation. Amen.

FOR GOD'S HELP AND STRENGTH

We beseech thee, Almighty God, look upon the hearty desires of thy humble servants, and stretch forth the right hand of thy majesty, to be our defense against all our enemies; through Jesus Christ our Lord. Amen.

O God, most wise and faithful Redeemer, who hast permitted us to come into this present trial: Grant that we may learn obedience by the things that we suffer, and turn to thee, our helper in the time of trouble. May there be no bitterness in our sorrow, no despair in our submission, and no doubt of thee in our perplexity. Teach us to face our trial bravely; make even the dark things of life to work together for our good; and bring us speedily out of our distress, that we may praise thee with a joyful heart; in Christ Jesus our Lord. Amen.

The Book of Prayers

IN LONELINESS

O heavenly Father, who wast with thy Son when all his companions were scattered: Be with me in my loneliness. Though I be far from my kindred and friends, join me to them in thy love and do for them what I dare not ask. Comfort us all with the presence of thy Son our Saviour, whom, through thy Holy Spirit, thou dost send to be the friend of all who are sad and forsaken. And so, at the last, O Lord, refresh my soul with gratitude for this loneliness, which now seemeth only to be grievous; for that, bringing me near to thee, it hath caused me to speak, and thou hast heard me and hast showed me marvellous great kindness in a strong city; through Jesus Christ our Lord. Amen.

FOR NEARNESS TO GOD

O Lord, by all thy dealings with us, whether of joy or pain, of light or darkness, let us be brought to thee. Let us value no treatment of thy grace simply because it makes us happy or because it makes us sad, because it gives us or denies us what we want; but may all that thou sendest us bring us to thee; that knowing thy perfectness we may be sure in every disappointment that thou art still loving us, and in every darkness that thou art still enlightening us, and in every enforced idleness thou art still using us; yea, in every death thou art giving us life, as in his death thou didst give life to thy Son, our Saviour Jesus Christ. Amen.

TO BE AT PEACE

Grant unto us, almighty God, thy peace that passeth understanding, that we, amid the sorrows of life, may rest in thee, knowing that all things are in thee, under thy care, governed by thy will, guarded by thy love, so that with a quiet heart we may face the clouds and the darkness, ever rejoicing to know that darkness and light are both alike to thee; through Jesus Christ our Lord. Amen.

ON FACING TEMPTATION

Lord and Master, Jesus Christ, who thyself wast tempted as we are, yet without sin: Give me grace to meet this temptation which now assails me and which I would overcome. Enable me to check all evil thoughts and passions, all enticements to self-indulgence or dishonest gain, and to find, like thee, my highest satisfactions in the doing of my heavenly Father's will. Amen.

FOR ENDURANCE

Lord Jesus, grant us daily grace for daily need; daily patience for a daily cross; daily, hourly, incessant love of thee to take up our cross and bear it after thee. We ask this for thine own Name's sake. Amen.

ON BEING UNEMPLOYED

O God, thou hast been my help in the days that are past. Turn not from me even now as I walk the streets, discouraged and disheartened, seeking work. Surely thou dost care for me. Guide me with thine eyes. Lead and direct me to find fit employment.

O Lord, my sins are ever before me. In my yesterdays I have not always served thee. Too often I have ignored thy goodness and thy mercy. Forgive me, and let me find peace for my soul in thee.

Take all resentment, bitterness, and rebellion out of my heart. Make me hopeful, cheerful, courageous, patient, and confident.

Thou hast promised to be with me in the day of trouble. Open thine hand and satisfy my needs. Teach me to face the day confident of thy goodness. O Lord, let me not doubt thy promises. Hear the cry of my distressed heart and disturbed mind. Have mercy upon me, for Jesus' sake. Amen.

BEFORE FACING AN UNPLEASANT SITUATION

O Lord, I beg thee to take away my dread of what I have to do; give me, I pray thee, grace to think and act in perfect charity, without regard to my own painful feelings but only considering what is thy will; for Jesus' sake. Amen.

XVI.

In Preparation for Death

THE NUMBERED DAYS

O God, who hast brought us to the last day of another week, our days and weeks glide swiftly away, reminding us of the night which is at hand when we shall cease from our earthly labors and lie down in the dust. Fit us for thy day, for thy house, and for thy glory; and grant that when the day of God shall dawn we may arise with joy and put on immortality, redeemed from all power of corruption, and made like unto the Son of God. Amen.

ON BEING PREPARED

I know, O Lord, that my life is drawing to a close; may death not find me unprepared but ready to pass into thy presence, trusting in the merits of thy Son Jesus Christ. Amen.

O Lord, on thy Cross thou didst cry, Father, into thy hands I commend my spirit. I, too, commend my spirit into his hands now when my end is near. Thou hast redeemed me, O faithful God. Amen.

FOR THE ABIDING PRESENCE OF GOD

As the quiet splendor of the day dies down, we wait for the shining of the light that never fades. We step aside from the crowded highway to seek the garden of the soul where thou keepest tryst for us at cool of day. We have looked into the worn faces of men, into the eyes of those who love us; and now we would look into the face of the Son of Man. We have dealt with the problems and labors of the world, and now we would walk awhile with thee, O Master, as friend walketh with friend, for counsel, for guidance, for strength and peace. Let thy peace be upon us. Call us from all that distracts; gather us into the quiet of thy love; meet us, O Father, for we seek thy face. Amen.

God of the morning and the twilight, Lord of birth and death, be with me now and at my departing. Go with me through all the days of my earthly journey as I seek to press toward the goal for the prize of thine upward call in Christ Jesus. Let me neither fear nor seek to hasten the day when I must say, It is finished. But keep me steadfast in the confidence that the times are in thy hands. Then when my work is done, let me go to dwell with thee in closer fellowship; through Christ our Lord who has led the way. Amen.

In Preparation for Death

Abide with me: fast falls the eventide;
The darkness deepens; Lord, with me abide:
When other helpers fail, and comforts flee,
Help of the helpless, O abide with me.

Hold thou thy Cross before my closing eyes:
Shine through the gloom, and point me to the skies:
Heaven's morning breaks, and earth's vain shadows flee:
In life, in death, O Lord, abide with me. Amen.

FOR A PEACEFUL DEATH

O Lord Jesus Christ, who by thy death didst take
away the sting of death: Grant unto us thy servants
so to follow in faith where thou hast led the way that
we may at length fall asleep peacefully in thee, and
awake up after thy likeness; through thy mercy, who
livest with the Father and the Holy Ghost, one God,
world without end. Amen.

XVII.
In Time of Mourning

FOR THOSE WHO MOURN

Almighty God, Father of mercies and giver of all comfort: Deal graciously, we pray thee, with all those who mourn, that, casting every care on thee, they may know the consolation of thy love; through Jesus Christ our Lord. Amen.

IN BEREAVEMENT

Almighty God, who hast taught us that they who mourn shall be comforted: Grant that in all our grief we may turn to thee; and, because our need is beyond the help of men, grant us the peace of thy consolation and the joy of thy love; through Jesus Christ our Lord. Amen.

O Lord, we pray thee, give us thy strength, that we may live more bravely and faithfully for the sake of those who are no longer with us here upon earth; and grant us so to serve thee day by day that we may find eternal fellowship with them; through him who died and rose again for us all, Jesus Christ our Lord. Amen.

In Time of Mourning

O God, from whom all good things do come, the author of all true and tender affections: Behold our broken hearts; behold our grief, whose depth is the measure of a love which was thy gift. Out of the deep we call upon thy Name, for there is mercy with thee, and in thy Word is our trust. Save us, O God, even while the waves of sorrow engulf us. Though we discern not thy full purpose, yet do we acknowledge that thou understandest all thy children. Teach us, therefore, to entrust to thine eternal keeping the deathless love which binds us to *him* whose going from our sight makes our heart faint within us. Steady us to hold with tranquil hand the candle of faith, a light in this our darkness, a flame undying amid the changes and chances of our mortality. So shall we honor *him* while we miss *him;* and so shall we permit thee to guide our steps along the hard path which lies before us, and which, if we are true, will reveal itself as the highway of the King who reigneth over heaven and earth, our Saviour Jesus Christ. Amen.

O thou who hast ordered this wondrous world and who knowest all things in earth and heaven: So fill our hearts with trust in thee that by night and by day, at all times and in all seasons, we may without fear commit those who are dear to us to thy never-failing love for this life and the life to come. Amen.

The Book of Prayers

THY WILL, NOT MINE, O LORD

O God, thou helper of the helpless, sustain and comfort every mourning heart. In thy holy keeping are the living and the dead; and all are safe till thou bring them to thine everlasting light. Give us strength to return to the quiet duties of our place. With chastened desires, with better aspirations, with truer diligence, with less trust in ourselves and more rest in thee, may we dedicate ourselves anew to the service of thy will, that, in the faith and Spirit of him who was made perfect through suffering, each of us may be ready to say, whenever the hour shall strike, Father, I have finished the work which thou gavest me to do. Amen.

FOR THOSE WHO HAVE LEFT THIS LIFE

O Father of all, we pray to thee for those whom we love but see no longer. Grant them thy peace; let light perpetual shine upon them; and, in thy loving wisdom and almighty power, work in them the good purpose of thy perfect will; through Jesus Christ our Lord. Amen.

ON THE DEATH OF A YOUNG MAN OR WOMAN

O Lord Jesus Christ, who hast known on earth the joy and vigor of youth, grant to *him* whom we love a welcome into thy service, that *he* may share with thee in the abundant life of thy eternal kingdom. Amen.

In Time of Mourning

ON THE DEATH OF A CHILD

Almighty Father, whose goodness loved us into life
and whose mercies never fail, thine is the beauty of
childhood and thine the light which shines in the face
of age. We bless thy holy Name for this child, recalling
all in *him* that made others love *him*. We praise thee
for all good and gracious influences with which thou
didst surround *him* and for all that ministered to *his*
joy and growth. In thy love and wisdom thou didst
give *him* a home of faith and tender care, and didst
nurture *him* by the fruits of the Spirit. For this we
render unto thee our gratitude. We thank thee that
even *his* brief life made *his* home and the circle of *his*
friends the more blessed for *his* presence; through
Jesus Christ our Lord. Amen.

Father of mercies and God of all comfort, be with
us in our grief. Let us not sorrow as those who have
no faith. Grant us steadfastly to believe that this child
has been taken into the safekeeping of thy eternal love,
and that thou art doing for *him* even more than we
could desire. This we ask in the Name of Jesus Christ.
Amen.

XVIII.

For the Church

FOR THE CHURCH

O Lord, we beseech thee, let thy continual pity cleanse and defend thy Church; and because it cannot continue in safety without thy succor, preserve it evermore by thy help and goodness; through Jesus Christ, thy Son our Lord, who liveth and reigneth with thee and the Holy Ghost, ever one God, world without end. Amen.

O gracious Father, we humbly beseech thee for thy world-wide Church of Christ, that thou wouldest be pleased to fill it with all truth, in all peace. Where it is corrupt, purify it; where it is in error, direct it; where in any thing it is amiss, reform it. Where it is right, establish it; where it is in want, provide for it; where it is divided, reunite it; for the sake of him who died and rose again, and ever liveth to make intercession for us, Jesus Christ thy Son our Lord. Amen.

Quicken, O Lord, we beseech thee, all the members of thy Church that they may be alive to the opportunities and responsibilities of these times. Save us from complacency and from fear of new ways; inspire our minds with the vision of a world won for thee, and stir our wills to pray and to work until thy will is done on earth as it is in heaven; for Jesus' sake. Amen.

FOR MINISTERS

O heavenly Father, remember all that do the Lord's work in the ministry. Give them, we beseech thee, O Father, great gifts and great holiness, that wisely and charitably, diligently and zealously, prudently and acceptably, they may be guides to the blind, comforters to the sad and weary; that they may strengthen the weak and confirm the strong; that in all their actions and ministrations they may advance the good of souls and the honor of our Lord Jesus Christ. Amen.

FOR CHURCH WORKERS

Almighty God, pour thy Holy Spirit upon all who are giving their lives to thy work. O Lord, take their minds and think through them; take their lips and speak through them; take their hearts and set them on fire with love of thee. Hear our prayer, O Lord of the harvest, and send forth more laborers into thy fields; in Jesus' Name. Amen.

FOR MISSIONS AND MISSIONARIES

Eternal Father, who art loving unto every man, and hast given thy Son to be the Saviour of the world:

Grant that the pure light of his Gospel may overcome the darkness of idolatry in every land and that all thy lost children, dwelling in far countries, may be brought home to thee. Protect the messengers of the Gospel amid all perils; guide them through all perplexities; give them wisdom, strength, and courage, to make known by word and life the grace of our Lord Jesus; prosper all that they do in his blessed Name, to serve the bodies and the souls of men; hasten, we beseech thee, the promised day, when at the Name of Jesus every knee shall bow and every tongue confess that he is Lord; to the glory of God the Father. Amen.

FOR CHURCH UNITY

O Lord and Father of us all, who didst send thy Son to be the Saviour of the world: Grant thy blessing to all the followers of Christ of every name and creed. May they rejoice in the privilege of being fellow workers with him and with each other, that the darkness of the world may be driven out by the Light of life. Deliver them from prejudice, from arrogance, and from contention. Bring them into close cooperation and harmony, that all their forces may be united for the common cause. Kindle in their hearts an increasing love for all Christians and a new desire to join with all sincere disciples of the Master in making his Gospel triumphant in all the earth. Grant that all the churches of Christ may seek a true Christian unity, that the captain of our salvation may lead his united hosts to victory in a world redeemed; through the same Jesus Christ our Lord. Amen.

O God, the Father of our Lord Jesus Christ, our only Saviour, the Prince of Peace: Give us grace seriously to lay to heart the great dangers we are in by our unhappy divisions. Take away all hatred and prejudice, and whatsoever else may hinder us from godly union and concord: that as there is but one Body and one Spirit, and one hope of our calling, one Lord, one faith, one baptism, one God and Father of us all, so we may be all of one heart and of one soul, united in one holy bond of truth and peace, of faith and charity, and may with one mind and one mouth glorify thee; through Jesus Christ our Lord. Amen.

XIX.

For the Kingdom of God on Earth

FOR THE KINGDOM

Almighty God, we pray thee for the coming of thy kingdom of righteousness and peace. In the midst of a changing social order may faith in thee and obedience to the teachings of thy dear Son prevail to build a new life of love in which the ills of this present time may disappear and the glad day of brotherhood and mutual service may dawn. Strengthen all the agencies of thy Church which are laboring for the happiness and welfare of all people that they may find in thee their salvation and their peace; through Jesus Christ our Lord. Amen.

FOR AN END TO BIGOTRY

O God, Creator of the world, Father of mankind: We thank thee for the blessing of life, for the joy of being thy sons. Inspire us, we pray thee, to faithful service in thy family on earth, make us to know the infinite debt we owe our fellow men, and let no pride of circumstance or narrowness of mind keep us from full and free communion with our brethren. And this we ask through the merits of him who called himself the Son of Man, Jesus Christ our Lord. Amen.

FOR THE WILL TO KEEP PEACE

O God, who hast put into the hearts of men a great longing for peace but hast also given to man the power to choose: Grant us the will to make our choices in accordance with thy will. Bind the world together, O God, in fellowship, service, and love, and grant that we may take our part in the fulfilment of thy purpose; through Jesus Christ our Lord. Amen.

FOR PEACE

O God, who through thy prophets of old hast foretold a day when the armaments of war shall be beaten into the implements of peace: Hasten, we beseech thee, the fulfilment of this thy most sure promise. Quell the haughty cries of the nations. Scatter the peoples that delight in war. Let counsels of peace and unity mightily prevail that we may be speedily delivered from our present confusion into the order and righteousness of thy kingdom; through Jesus Christ our Lord. Amen.

Eternal God, in whose will is our peace: We cry unto thee for the ending of war and of preparations for war. O make haste, we beseech thee, to save us, lest our cities become heaps and we be left desolate and despairing, going into the holes of the rocks and into the caves of the earth for fear of destruction. In thy mercy turn us from the things that make for discord, division, and strife.

Deliver us from self-righteousness, from foolish pride and boasting, and from all contempt of others.

Deliver us from the desire to impose our will upon others and from consent to reap benefit at others' expense.

Deliver us from putting our trust in bombs and battleships, while neglecting the demands of thy righteousness, the ways of thy mercy, and the adventures of thy faith.

O thou who rulest the world from end to end and from everlasting to everlasting, make us to know that thou art God and that in thee alone is our hope. Grant us grace to repent of our sins and to yield our wills to thine, that thou mayest forgive all our iniquities and heal all our diseases and redeem our lives from destruction. Bring us more and more into fellowship with thee, O God of peace, that we may have peace within our hearts and that thou, O Lord, mayest work through us to give peace to the world; through Jesus Christ our Lord. Amen.

Almighty God, from whom all thoughts of truth and peace proceed: Kindle, we pray thee, in the hearts of all men the true love of peace and guide with thy pure and peaceable wisdom those who take counsel for the nations of the earth that in tranquility thy kingdom may go forward till the earth be filled with the knowledge of thy love; through Jesus Christ our Lord. Amen.

FOR A BETTER WORLD

O God, the father of all mankind, we beseech thee to guide by thy Spirit the nations of the world. May selfishness be overcome by a desire to serve the common good. Grant to rulers and nations wisdom, patience, and strength to know and to do thy will, that peace and justice may be established among us for all generations. Amen.

Almighty God, in whose hand are all the nations of the earth, grant to them all thy guidance and help that they may seek prosperity in promoting the welfare of their people and of all mankind. Grant to all peoples and races that they may feel their kinship with each other since all men are alike the children of the same eternal Father. Restrain them from jealousy, hatred, and selfish ambition. Awaken in them the spirit of justice, fraternity, and concord. Unite them by the bonds of international friendship that they may work together for the betterment of the whole world. Make wars to cease, and hasten the day when there shall be everywhere peace on earth and good will among men; this we ask in the name of the Prince of Peace. Amen.

Almighty God, our heavenly Father: Guide, we beseech thee, the nations of the world into the way of justice and truth, and establish among them that peace which is the fruit of righteousness; that they may become the kingdom of our Lord and Saviour, Jesus Christ. Amen.

FOR A JUST AND PEACEFUL WORLD ORDER

O God, who art the author of peace and lover of concord, we thank thee for the nations which have pledged themselves to seek the settlement of their disputes only by peaceful means. We pray thee that in their counsels they may have the guidance of thy Holy Spirit of wisdom and truth, so that mindful of their promise they may live at peace in a commonwealth of nations, according to thy will; through Jesus Christ our Lord. Amen.

O Lord Jesus Christ, who biddest thy Church to bring all men to thyself: Make clear to each one of us his part in the task. Fire our minds with a vision of a more perfect society here on earth in which justice and right, peace and brotherhood shall reign according to thy will, and help us, each one, O Lord, to do our part, that thy will may be done on earth as it is in heaven. Amen.

FOR THE BROTHERHOOD OF MAN

Bind, O God, the heart of every man to his neighbor, and the hearts of all men to thee, in whom thy family in heaven and earth are one; through the power of the Holy Ghost. Amen.

O Lord Jesus Christ, who art the light of the world: Let the sun of thy righteousness, we pray thee, arise in our hearts, to burn away the barriers that separate us from our fellow men; for thine is the kingdom, world without end. Amen.

O God, who hast made man in thine own likeness and who dost love all whom thou hast made: Teach us the unity of thy family and the breadth of thy love. By the example of thy Son, Jesus our Saviour, enable us, while loving and serving our own, to enter into the fellowship of the whole human family, and forbid that, from pride of race or hardness of heart, we should despise any for whom Christ died or injure any in whom he lives. Amen.

XX.

Calendar of Prayer

THE NEW YEAR

Almighty and everlasting God, from whom cometh down every good and perfect gift: We give thee thanks for all thy benefits, temporal and spiritual, bestowed upon us in the year past; and, we beseech thee, of thy goodness, grant us a favorable and joyful year, defend us from all dangers and adversities, and send upon us the fullness of thy blessing; through Jesus Christ, thy Son our Lord, who liveth and reigneth with thee and the Holy Ghost, ever one God, world without end. Amen.

Eternal God, who hast revealed thyself to the ever-changing lives of men in a Word that stands fast forever: Speak now to our hearts as we wait here on the threshold of changing years. Remind us of all thy mercies which have shown forth thy love, and turn our faces toward thy coming. For every fleeting glimpse we have had of thy glory, for every prompting of conscience, for the light that shines on the pathway of duty, for the reasonableness of faith and the persistence of hope, for all thy bounty in the past and for every promise thou hast made for the future, we thank thee—for the dreams we have had, and the voice we hear, the presence and power of thy Spirit like the breath of wind on water, for the Christ whose daily companionship unites our lives, we thank thee.

We confess our unworthiness before thee. Forgive us, we pray thee, and be gracious to us still. Trouble us anew with thy Word and Presence. Torment us until we die with the difference between what we are and what thou wouldest have us be.

Hold before our eyes that pure will of thine until we learn to choose it above all the wealth and esteem of the world. Establish us again in the truth which we have known so long yet ever comes to us from the lips of Jesus like freshly awakened memories. Restore in us all that we have believed and lost awhile—planned once when life was at its morning but given over now —until once more we find joy for our sorrow, and for our weakness a strength that is not our own. Enter into our lives, and prove thyself with the beauty which we may yet make familiar on earth. Give us of the mind and heart of Christ and, whatever it may cost, of thy goodness, peace at the end of our days.

Send us now to our tasks again. What thou hast planted in our hearts, through the days to come, bring to our lips in praise and to our hands in compassion.

Teach us to speak kindly, act gently, bear ourselves gladly and hopefully, asking of thee no more than thou wilt ever freely give, and ever, in the asking, pledging thee our faith and eager obedience; through Jesus Christ our Lord, to whom with thee and the Holy Ghost be glory and dominion both now and ever. Amen.

O thou, who art ever the same, grant us so to pass through the coming year with faithful hearts that we may be able in all things to please thy loving eyes; for Jesus' sake. Amen.

EPIPHANY

O God, who by the guidance of a star didst this day reveal thine only-begotten Son to the nations: Mercifully grant that we, who know thee now by faith, may be so guided as to behold with our eyes the beauty of thy majesty; through Jesus Christ our Lord. Amen.

ASH WEDNESDAY

Almighty and everlasting God, who hatest nothing that thou hast made, and dost forgive the sins of all those who are penitent: Create and make in us new and contrite hearts that we, worthily lamenting our sins and acknowledging our wretchedness, may obtain of thee, the God of all mercy, perfect remission and forgiveness; through Jesus Christ our Lord. Amen.

LENT

Almighty God, who seest that we have no power of ourselves to help ourselves: Keep us both outwardly in our bodies and inwardly in our souls, that we may be defended from all adversities which may happen to the body and from all evil thoughts which may assault and hurt the soul; through Jesus Christ our Lord. Amen.

O Lord our Master, who through the forty days didst forget the body because thy Spirit was caught up in God: Teach us with whole hearts to seek thy heavenly communion, so that being delivered from subjection to the flesh we may be released into the spiritual liberty that belongs to the children of God. In thine own Name we ask it. Amen.

Almighty God, who givest us our quiet seasons of thought and prayer, help us now and at all times to find in thee our true peace. Save us in the hour of trial, deliver us from evil thoughts and desires and from the tyranny of outward things. May we learn of Christ to be strong and brave in the struggle with temptation and to overcome even as he overcame. Amen.

The Book of Prayers

PALM SUNDAY

Our Father, as on this day we celebrate our Redeemer's entry into Jerusalem, so grant, O Lord, that now and ever he may triumph in our hearts. Let the King of grace and glory enter in, that we may lay ourselves and all we are in full and joyful homage before him; through the same Jesus Christ our Lord. Amen.

GOOD FRIDAY

Almighty God, who in the life and teaching of thy Son hast showed us the true way of blessedness: Thou hast also showed us in his sufferings and death that the path of duty may lead to the Cross and the reward of faithfulness may be a crown of thorns. Give us grace to learn these harder lessons. May we take up our cross and follow Christ in the strength of patience and the constancy of faith; and may we have such fellowship with him in his sorrow that we may know the secret of his strength and peace, and see, even in our darkest hour of trial and anguish, the shining of the eternal light. Amen.

O Lord Jesus Christ, who for our sakes didst suffer death upon the Cross: Help us to bear about with us thy dying and, in our living, to show forth thy life. Looking on thee whom we have pierced, we would mourn for our sins with unfeigned sorrow; we would learn of thee to forgive, with thee to suffer, and in thee to overcome. Lamb of God, who takest away the sins of the world, have mercy upon us. Lamb of God, who takest away the sins of the world, grant us thy peace. Lord, we pray thee, in thy great mercy, remember us when thou comest into thy kingdom. Amen.

HOLY WEEK

Almighty God, whose most dear Son went not up to joy but first he suffered pain, and entered not into glory before he was crucified: Mercifully grant that we, walking in the way of the Cross, may find it none other than the way of life and peace; through the same, thy Son Jesus Christ our Lord. Amen.

EASTER

O God, who for our redemption didst give thine only-begotten Son to the death of the Cross and by his glorious resurrection hast delivered us from the power of our enemy: Grant us so to die daily from sin that we may evermore live with him in the joy of his resurrection; through the same, thy Son Christ our Lord. Amen.

Almighty Father, who through the eternal victory of thy Son hast brought us through the shadow of the Cross and the gloom of the garden and the night of the tomb to the glorious sunrise of everlasting light and life: Fill us with the glory of his victory, so that transformed and strengthened by him we may overcome all that separates us from thee in this life, and through him come to the life that never ends. Amen.

O God, who, through the mighty resurrection of thy Son Jesus Christ from the dead, hast delivered us from the power of darkness into the kingdom of thy love: Grant, we beseech thee, that as by his death he has recalled us into life, so, by his presence ever abiding in us, he may raise us to joys eternal; through him who for our sakes died and rose again, and is ever with us in power and great glory; even the same Jesus Christ our Lord. Amen.

ASCENSION DAY

O God, the King of glory, who hast exalted thine only Son Jesus Christ with great triumph unto thy kingdom in heaven: We beseech thee, leave us not comfortless, but send to us thine Holy Ghost to comfort us and exalt us unto the same place whither our Saviour Christ is gone before, who liveth and reigneth with thee and the same Holy Ghost, one God, world without end. Amen.

WHITSUNTIDE

Send, we beseech thee, almighty God, thy Holy Spirit into our hearts, that he may rule and direct us according to thy will, comfort us in all our temptations and afflictions, defend us from all error, and lead us into all truth; that we, being steadfast in the faith, may increase in love and in all good works, and in the end obtain everlasting life; through Jesus Christ thy Son our Lord. Amen.

O God, who wast pleased to send upon thy disciples the Holy Spirit, in the burning fire of thy love: Grant to us thy people to be fervent in the unity of the Spirit, that evermore, abiding in thee, we may be found both steadfast in faith and active in work; through Jesus Christ our Lord. Amen.

MEMORIAL DAY

Lord God of Hosts, in whom our fathers trusted: We give thee thanks for all thy servants who have laid down their lives in the service of our country. Unite all the people of this nation in a holy purpose to defend the freedom and brotherhood for which they lived and died. Grant, we beseech thee, that the liberty they bequeathed unto us may be continued to our children and our children's children, and that the power of the Gospel may here abound, to the blessing of all the nations of the earth, and to thine eternal glory; through Jesus Christ thy Son our Lord. Amen.

TRINITY SUNDAY

O Lord God Almighty, eternal, immortal, invisible, the mysteries of whose being are unsearchable: Accept, we beseech thee, our praises for the revelation which thou hast made of thyself, Father, Son, and Holy Ghost, three Persons, and one God; and mercifully grant that ever holding fast this faith, we may magnify thy glorious Name; who livest and reignest, one God, world without end. Amen.

INDEPENDENCE DAY

O eternal God, through whose mighty power our fathers won their liberties of old: Grant, we beseech thee, that we and all the people of this land may have grace to maintain these liberties in righteousness and peace; through Jesus Christ our Lord. Amen.

LABOR DAY

Almighty Father, who by thy Son Jesus Christ hast sanctified labor to the welfare of mankind: Prosper, we pray thee, the industries of this land and all those who are engaged therein that, shielded in all their temptations and dangers, and receiving a due reward of their labors, they may praise thee by living according to thy will; through Jesus Christ our Lord. Amen.

Calendar of Prayer

BIBLE SUNDAY

O Lord God, heavenly Father, we beseech thee so to rule and guide us by thy Holy Spirit that we may hear and receive thy holy Word with our whole heart, in order that through thy Word we also may be sanctified and may learn to place all our trust and hope in Jesus Christ thy Son, and following him may be led safely in the face of all evil, until by thy grace we come to everlasting life; through the same Jesus Christ thy Son our Lord. Amen.

O Lord, heavenly Father, in whom is the fullness of light and wisdom: Enlighten our minds by thy Holy Spirit and give us grace to receive thy Word with reverence and humility, without which no man can understand thy truth. For Jesus Christ's sake. Amen.

ALL SAINTS' DAY

We give thanks to thee, O Lord, for all saints and servants of thine, who have done justly, loved mercy, and walked humbly with their God. For all the high and holy ones, who have wrought wonders and been shining lights in the world, we thank thee. For all the meek and lowly ones, who have earnestly sought thee in darkness, and held fast their faith in trial, and done good unto all men as they had opportunity, we thank thee. Especially for those men and women whom we

The Book of Prayers

have known and loved, who by their patient obedience and self-denial, steadfast hope and helpfulness in trouble, have shown the same mind that was in Christ Jesus, we bless thy holy Name. As they have comforted and upheld our souls, grant us grace to follow in their steps, and at last to share with them in the inheritance of the saints in light; through Jesus Christ our Saviour. Amen.

THANKSGIVING DAY

Almighty and everlasting God, who hast graciously given to us the fruits of the earth in their season: We yield thee humble and hearty thanks for these thy bounties, beseeching thee to give us grace rightly to use them to thy glory and the relief of those that need; through Jesus Christ our Lord. Amen.

Almighty God, our heavenly Father, from whom cometh every good and perfect gift: Let thy blessing rest upon us in this festival of thanksgiving. We praise thee as the bountiful benefactor from whose gracious hand all our blessings have come. We remember thy loving-kindness and tender mercy toward us through all the years, and with grateful hearts we lift up to thee our songs of joy. For all the gifts thou hast bestowed upon us, and upon our land, and upon the whole family of man, we give thee humble and hearty thanks. May we show our gratitude by faithful lives devoted to thy service; through Jesus Christ our Lord. Amen.

ADVENT

Almighty God, give us grace that we may cast away the works of darkness and put upon us the armor of light, now in the time of this mortal life, in which thy Son Jesus Christ came to visit us in great humility; that in the last day, when he shall come again, in his glorious, majesty to judge both the quick and the dead, we may rise to the life immortal; through him who liveth and reigneth with thee and the Holy Ghost, now and ever. Amen.

Almighty God, our heavenly Father, who didst cause light to shine out of darkness in the advent of our Lord Jesus Christ, to take away the sins of the world: We humbly confess our transgressions and implore thy forgiveness. We beseech thee that the Spirit of Christ may be born anew within us, and that we may glorify his nativity with hearts of compassion, deeds of kindly service, and the spirit of good will toward all mankind; through Jesus Christ our Lord. Amen.

CHRISTMAS

We commit unto thee, O God, in this silent hour, all our Christmas plans, our hopes, our daily work, our families and family reunions, our gaieties and our griefs, asking thy blessing upon every thought and endeavor, thy control over every enterprise, thy spirit of charity in our hearts and wisdom in our minds, that when thy Son our Lord cometh he may find in us a mansion prepared for himself; through the same, our Saviour Jesus Christ. Amen.

O Almighty God, who by the birth of thy holy child Jesus hast given us a great light to dawn upon our darkness: Grant, we pray thee, that in his light we may see light to the end of our days; and bestow upon us, we beseech thee, that most excellent Christmas gift of charity to all men, so that the likeness of thy Son may be formed in us and that we may have the ever-brightening hope of everlasting life; through Jesus Christ our Lord. Amen.

O God, of heavenly glory, source of earthly peace and good will: May our Christmas be merry because touched with joy divine; through him who in his purity and love is born in our hearts today, thy son Jesus Christ our Lord. Amen.

XXI.

Of Home and Among Friends

FOR FRIENDS AND NEIGHBORS

O thou who art the God of all the families of the earth, bless, I pray thee, all our friends and neighbors. Watch over their homes and shield them from all harm and evil. Protect their dwellings from fire, from thieves, and from anything that would destroy them or bring them trouble. Help me to be thoughtful for their welfare and the protection of their property. Show me how I can serve them. Make me a ready and willing friend and a true neighbor; for Jesus' sake. Amen.

FOR A FRIEND WHO HAS LOST A PARENT

Heavenly Father, help me to be thankful that thou hast continued my home to me. Remember my friend whose home is broken. Show thyself very near to *him* and be to *him* more than a father or a mother. Help me to stand by *him* in *his* sorrow and show me how I can comfort *him*. Help us all to think more of thee and of thy heavenly home; and may we not fail, through any sin of ours, to meet our loved ones there. For Jesus' sake. Amen.

FOR LOYALTY TO FRIENDS

O God, Father and friend of all: Teach me how to be a good friend. Help me to be loyal and true to those who love and trust me. Make me the kind of person on whom my friends may depend at all times. For Jesus' sake. Amen.

OF THANKSGIVING FOR HOME

Heavenly Father, I praise thee for thy mercy in giving me a good home. When I was a helpless child my parents cared for me, and by their love all my needs have been supplied. When I am tempted to be impatient of the restraints of my home, help me to remember Jesus who was subject to his parents. Keep me from a sullen and ungrateful spirit. Show me how I may help to make my home a blessing to all who come to it, and let the law of kindness rule my life. For thy Name's sake. Amen.

Of Home and Among Friends

FOR A HAPPY HOME

O God, who makest of one mind men that live in a house together, bring peace into our home. Help me to do my share. Make me ever ready to give the understanding answer that turneth away wrath. Take from me the wish to irritate, and prevent me from saying the grievous words that stir up strife. If I am tempted to quarrel, make me able to keep my own temper. Let the law of kindness rule my life and govern all I do and say. When my feelings are hurt, let me turn to thee for comfort, and keep me calm under the shadow of thy wings; for Jesus' sake. Amen.

FOR HONOR

Grant, O God, that we may never bring sorrow or unhappiness to our parents or to our friends. Help us to keep to the standard that those who love us have lifted, and in all things help us to bring honor and respect to our family name. Amen.

FOR LOVE OF OTHERS

O God, help me to be unselfish. Help me to be courteous to my parents, to my teachers, to my friends, and to all. Help me to sacrifice my comfort for others. Make me kindly and thoughtful in word and generous in deed. Help me to learn that it is better to forget self than to put self first. Help me to live in the spirit of

Jesus who went about doing good and laid down his life for others. For his sake. Amen.

OF THANKSGIVING FOR PARENTS

Lord, we thank thee for our fathers and mothers and for their labors in our behalf. Bless them with long life and grant us grace to give them joy by what we do and say. In Jesus' Name. Amen.

XXII.

Of the World of School and Scholarship

FOR SCHOOL OR COLLEGE

O God, we pray thee to send thy blessing upon this school and grant that by the help of thy Holy Spirit we may strive with one heart and mind to make this place more and more pleasing to thee; for the honor and glory of thy Son, our Saviour Jesus Christ. Amen.

Almighty God, our heavenly Father, who art the only source of light and life, send down upon this school the rich gifts of thy good Spirit that thy truth may be sincerely sought, faithfully received, and obediently followed.

Endue its teachers with wisdom, zeal, and patience. Inspire its scholars with the spirit of truth, honor, and humility. May they, day by day, grow in grace and in the knowledge of our Lord and Saviour, Jesus Christ.

Grant to all in this school such a cheerful and forbearing spirit, such strength of body, clearness of mind, and purity of heart that thy work may be heartily done and thy Name glorified.

Let thy blessing rest upon us now and thy Spirit dwell in this place from generation to generation; through thy Son our Lord and Saviour Jesus Christ. Amen.

O God, who art the fountain of wisdom and the inspiration of knowledge: We beseech thee to inspire and prosper this school in all its work and grant that by our diligence and faithfulness true religion and useful learning may abound to the good of mankind and the glory of thy great Name; through Jesus Christ our Lord. Amen.

FOR TEACHERS AND STUDENTS

Grant, O Lord, to all teachers and students to know that which is worth knowing, to love that which is worth loving, to praise that which pleaseth thee most, and to dislike whatsoever is evil in thine eyes. Grant us with true judgment to distinguish things that differ, and above all to search out and to do what is well-pleasing unto thee; through Jesus Christ our Lord. Amen.

AT THE BEGINNING OF THE TERM

O God, our help in times past: Be with us as we enter upon this new term. Pour down upon us thy grace that we may enter fully into the life of the school, pursuing our studies with diligence and engaging whole-heartedly in our activities. Help us at all times to be manly and truthful, courageous and unselfish in our dealings with our fellows. And this we beg for Jesus Christ's sake. Amen.

BEFORE STUDY

Grant me, I beseech thee, O merciful God, ardently to desire, prudently to study, mightily to understand, and perfectly to fulfil that which is pleasing to thee; to the praise and glory of thy Name. Amen.

Almighty God, who art the source of all wisdom: Prosper and direct me in my studies that they may redound to thy glory and to my eternal good; through Jesus Christ our Lord. Amen.

O God, who hast ordained that whatever is to be desired should be sought by labor, and who by thy blessing bringest honest labor to good effect: Look with favor upon our studies and endeavors; grant us, O Lord, to design only what is right and lawful, that in humility of mind we may see the truth and in gentleness of heart may serve our generation. Amen.

Grant, O Lord, we pray thee, that as we seek for truth we may find that the search leads us to thee. Give us courage to seek honestly and reverence to seek humbly and, when our minds are perplexed and we cannot find thee, give us patience to go on with our daily duties; through Jesus Christ our Lord. Amen.

FOR A BETTER USE OF TIME

O God, who hast appointed unto man but a short span of life and opportunity: I pray thee, help me to make use of my time here at school and to value the fleeting hours for which I must render an account to thee. May I overcome idleness and indolence and apply myself wholeheartedly to my work, ever redeeming the time, both for my own benefit and for the good of the school; through Jesus Christ our Lord. Amen.

O God, all my life is thine. Help me so to plan and arrange the hours of this day that I may serve thee in them all, for they are thine. Amen.

FOR A WISE USE OF KNOWLEDGE

O God of all wisdom and knowledge: Teach us to know that every discovery of truth is a discovery of thee and that the more we learn of thy laws and thy ways among men the nearer we are brought to an understanding of thy divine being; through Jesus Christ our Lord. Amen.

Almighty God, who hast given to men the capacity to search out and use the wonderful powers of thy universe: Grant to us also the sense of responsibility and the wisdom to use those powers not for destruction but for the benefit of all mankind. For the sake of Jesus Christ our Lord. Amen.

FOR AN OPEN MIND

Give me an open mind, O God, a mind ready to receive and to welcome such new light of knowledge as it is thy will to reveal to me. Let not the past ever be so dear as to set a limit to the future. Give me courage to change my mind, when that is needed. Let me be tolerant to the thoughts of others and hospitable to such light as may come to me through them. In Jesus' Name. Amen.

FOR THE ADVANCEMENT OF SCIENCE

O God, who art the giver of every good and perfect gift: Grant thine aid to all who carry on the work of research. Bestow both skill and learning on those who are seeking to understand the mysteries of nature for the good of their fellow men. Reward their patient labors and their willing exposure to unknown risks by granting them an abundant harvest of useful discovery and an increase of knowledge; through Jesus Christ our Lord. Amen.

BEFORE AN ATHLETIC EVENT

O Lord, in all our games help us to quit ourselves like men, playing fair with our opponents, giving of the best that is in us to our side, and always placing the name and the honor of the school above the victory; through Jesus Christ our Lord and Friend. Amen.

BEFORE AN EXAMINATION

O God, be with me today and help me to do my best. Give me a clear mind and an honest heart. If there are things I do not know, let me not be flustered or afraid but let me use to the utmost what I do know. May everything in which I have worked hard stand by me now and, if in anything I must face the results of laziness, make me resolve to work better in the days ahead. Help me to express all I know; but whether I can do that or not, grant that I may have learned something that will last; through Jesus Christ my Lord. Amen.

AT THE CLOSE OF THE SCHOOL YEAR

Keep us, O Lord, we beseech thee, as we go forth from this place, and preserve in us the recollection of thy continual presence. Be with those who are leaving school and guide them on their way; strengthen with thy Spirit those who are to return that in all the thoughts and actions of their daily lives they may live worthy of their calling and be ready to serve thee with new life and hope, to the glory of thy Name; through Jesus Christ our Lord. Amen.

Of the World of School and Scholarship

Almighty and eternal God, by whose will our lives were brought into being, by whose Word we are upheld, and in whose Presence we stand, blessed be thy holy Name for this that thou hast willed and spoken concerning us. Thou hast gathered us into families, led us by thy work and ways into the fellowship of them that believe, and called us by name into thy service, ever ready by thy Spirit to fit us each to his task in thy kingdom.

For the love we have had, for the opportunities with which thou hast provided us, for the friendships that have been formed, and for the hopes that have been born of thee, we thank thee; for every prompting of conscience and for every vision of the truth which thou hast revealed to us in Christ, we thank thee.

All of this we would this day dedicate anew to thee. Look with thy favor upon us as we give into thy keeping against the coming years the gifts thou hast given us. Renew in us, at a deeper level than knowledge, that faith which is the present evidence of things not seen. For our weakness, grant us strength which is not our own. Speak thyself in the words we speak. Grant us with honesty and fearlessness to think after thee thy thoughts. Work thou in our work. Let no good promise we have made be broken, nor any wrong we have done, or any we shall see, continue for want of the good that would repair it. And forasmuch as thou dost use for thy mighty purpose such lives as, in gratitude, are offered unto thee, channel through us thy grace and some portion of thine own divine intent; through Jesus Christ our Lord, to whom with thee and the Holy Ghost be glory and dominion both now and ever. Amen.

BEFORE A VACATION

Grant, O Lord, that we may so enjoy our holiday at this season that our bodies may be strengthened, our minds renewed, and our energies quickened, for the perfect freedom of thy service; through Jesus Christ our Lord. Amen.

FOR FORTITUDE IN FAILURE

O God, thou art the strength of all who put their trust in thee. Help me not to be cast down by my defeat. If the fault was mine, help me to know my weaknesses and to do better another time. Help me to learn that failure may be a blessing if it leads to perseverance. Help me to learn that lesson now and give me strength to try again. For Jesus' sake. Amen.

XXIII.

Of Patriotism

FOR COUNTRY

We thank thee, Father, for the freedom and opportunities we have in our land. It is all from thee, for thou hast blessed us far above what we deserve. Keep us, as a people, in thy fear, and grant to us and those who rule over us thy guidance and protection; for Jesus' sake. Amen.

OF DEDICATION TO CHURCH AND COUNTRY

O heavenly Father, who hast blessed us with Christian homes and a free country: Give us a deeper sense of thy goodness and arouse in us a greater love of thee and of thy service. By thy Spirit move us to be more helpful to our home, our church, our country, and to everyone near and far, and to follow loyally in the steps of thy Son our Saviour Jesus Christ. Amen.

FOR GOOD CITIZENSHIP

O Lord, our heavenly Father, we pray thee to direct us into a life of service for our fellow men. Fill us with such wisdom, patience, and courage that we may become fearless and steadfast Christian citizens, and teach us to use our freedom to advance thy kingdom; for the sake of him who laid down his life for us, thy Son Jesus Christ. Amen.

FOR SOCIAL JUSTICE

O Lord, we pray that thou wilt hasten the time when no man shall live in contentment while he knows that his neighbor has need. Inspire in us and in all men the consciousness that we are not our own but thine and our neighbor's; for his sake, who prayed that we might all be one in him, Christ Jesus our Lord. Amen.

FOR WORLD PEACE

O God, the Father in heaven: Grant thy mighty aid to the efforts of men to establish peace among the nations of the world. Give strength of purpose to those who lead, enlighten those who sit in council, and so transform the hearts of men everywhere by thy gracious Gospel that they may exalt peace above war, service above gain, and righteousness above glory; through Jesus Christ our Lord. Amen.

XXIV.

For Finding
a Place in Life

FOR A PURPOSE IN LIFE

O God, who hast called me to thy service: Show me thy purpose for my life. Though it be hard, make me long to follow it, and give me courage to persevere till, at the last, I reach the goal which thou hast set for me; through Jesus Christ our Lord. Amen.

O Lord Jesus Christ, who hast made me and redeemed me and brought me where I am upon my way: Thou knowest what thou wouldest do with me; do according to thy will, with mercy. Amen.

FOR OPPORTUNITIES TO SERVE

Send us, O God, as thy messengers, to hearts without a home, to lives without love, to the crowds without a guide. Send us to the children whom none has blessed, to the famished whom none has visited, to the fallen whom none has lifted, to the bereaved whom none has comforted. Kindle thy flame on the altars of our

[139]

hearts that others may be warmed thereby, cause thy light to shine in our souls that others may see the way, and ever keep our sympathies and insight ready, our wills keen, and our hands quick to help our brothers in their need; through Jesus Christ our Lord. Amen.

FOR GUIDANCE ON LIFE'S WAY

Our God and Father, show us thy way: Grant that we may not blindly choose our own and so miss our goal. We thank thee for all signs of warning and guidance, and pray for obedient hearts that we may follow them. In Jesus' Name. Amen.

O God, heavenly Father, give me thy blessing as I face the tasks of life. With all my getting of knowledge, give me wisdom. Help me not to lead a small life in a great generation, in a great world, under a great God, with great issues at stake. Enlarge my vision of the needs of humanity and give me an unselfish spirit that I may make of life not a trade but an art and a cause; through Jesus Christ our Lord. Amen.

FOR A VOCATION

Show me, O Lord, what my life's work is to be. Help me to find what I can do best and prepare me for it now in mind and body; through Jesus Christ our Lord. Amen.

For Finding a Place in Life

FOR WORK

O God, who hast ordained that man should work for daily bread, show me the work that is appointed for me to do. Thou knowest the things that I need. Help me to find the honest task that will make me able to get them. Let me not despise my task, even if it be small, but help me to do it so well that I may obtain a better one. I am part of this great world thou hast made. Give me a place in its work that I may have enough for my own needs and be able to help those who have less. I ask this for the sake of thy Son Jesus Christ, who worked with his hands when he was on earth. Amen.

XXV.
Daily Prayers

IN THE MORNING

This is the day which thou hast made. I will rejoice and be glad in it. I give thanks unto thee, O Lord, for thy great goodness to me, to mine, and to all mankind. Amen.

Thou knowest, O heavenly Father, the duties that lie before me this day, the dangers that may confront me, the sins that most beset me. Guide me, strengthen me, protect me.

Give me thy power that I may become a power for righteousness among my fellows. Let me find thy power, thy love, thy life, in all mankind, and in the secret places of my own soul. Amen.

Today, O Lord, let me put
Right before interest,
Others before self,
The things of the Spirit before the things of the body,
The attainment of noble ends above the enjoyment of
       present pleasures,
Principle above reputation, and

Thee before all else;
Through Jesus Christ my Lord. Amen.

AT NOON

O Lord, do not let a busy life turn me from thy service. Make and keep me thine. For Jesus' sake. Amen.

IN THE EVENING

O Lord our God, refresh us with quiet sleep when we are wearied with the day's work, that, being assisted with the help which our weakness needs, we may be devoted to thee both in body and mind; through Jesus Christ our Lord. Amen.

We give thee thanks, O Lord, who hast kept us through the day. We give thee thanks, who wilt keep us through the night. Bring us, we beseech thee, O Lord, in safety to the morning of another day, that thou mayest receive our praise at all times; through Jesus Christ our Lord. Amen.

O heavenly Father, make us sorry for all the wrong things that we have done, and help us to grow better every day. Keep us from all meanness and selfishness and from hurting others by word or deed. Help us gladly to obey our parents and teachers; make us painstaking and cheerful in doing every duty. Help us to be more reverent and attentive in church and school. May we be always pure and truthful and learn day by day to know thee better and to love thee more. And bring us all at the end into thine everlasting kingdom; through Jesus Christ our Lord. Amen.

O God, our heavenly Father, thou hast freely given us all things. Thou hast made the world beautiful. Thou dost send the sunshine and the rain that the earth may yield us food and flowers. Thou hast given us the homes we love and hast set us among many friends. All day long we are safe in thy keeping, and at night we sleep in peace because of thy gracious care.

We thank thee, our Father, for all these gifts of thy bounty. As thou dost love us, so may we, by loving and helping others, show ourselves thy grateful children; through Jesus Christ our Lord. Amen.

Take us, we pray thee, O Lord of our life, into thy keeping this night and forever. O thou Light of lights, keep us from inward darkness; grant us so to sleep in peace that we may arise to work according to thy will; through Jesus Christ our Lord. Amen.

God, be merciful to me, for I know that I have failed thee. I knew better and still I did wrong. Forgive me, O my Father, and give me thy grace and strength to start again in new hope and trust; through Jesus Christ our Lord. Amen.

[144]

XXVI.

For Character and Spiritual Growth

ON A BIRTHDAY

O Lord God, who hast created all things, thou art the author of my being and through Jesus Christ thou art my Father. Thou hast blessed me in many ways and with many good things, and thou hast mercifully kept me to the present hour. For all this I thank thee. Forgive me graciously all the sins done in the days that are past; and, as I enter upon a new year of life, give me thy Holy Spirit to be my guide, that I may ever walk in the light of thy countenance according to thy Word. Amen.

AT CONFIRMATION

O God, whose child I was made in holy baptism, be with me and bless me in my confirmation. As I renew the vows that were made for me and make my promise to follow Jesus Christ as my Lord and Saviour, may thy

Holy Spirit give me strength to keep my promise and the will to be a loyal member of the Church all the days of my life; through Jesus Christ our Lord. Amen.

FOR A CONSECRATED LIFE

Eternal God, who art the author of our life, we do thank thee for this gift. Grant that we may ever cherish it as a high and sacred trust. Without thee we can do nothing but with thee all things are possible. Awaken in us the realization that thou hast a purpose for each to fulfil, that life is filled with sacred meaning, and that thou art the God of the inner summons, of quiet confidence, and of enduring companionship.

Bestow upon us a rich measure of thy wisdom that we may take from our past experiences insight that will serve us in the present hour. Guide us in our choices that we may weigh them in the light of future possibilities. Keep us from neglect of soul that we may finish our course in a manner that is well pleasing unto thee.

Bestow upon us a portion of thy concern for all men that we may never be indifferent to the rights and needs of others. Keep us ever close to him who came not to be ministered unto but to minister. In this great and challenging generation, let us never become little persons. We bring our wills to be strengthened until our purposes are undergirded by thy purpose. We bring our minds, open and receptive to thy truth, that we may know freedom. We bring our hearts to be quickened,

For Character and Spiritual Growth

until our love meets and mingles with thy love, that they may become a kingdom wherein we may walk in large and great places, reflecting some measure of the Spirit of him who is the Way, the Truth, and the Life. In Jesus' name. Amen.

FOR HONESTY

O God, whose eyes behold the hidden secrets of the heart, help me to be honest in thy sight and before all men. Make me sincere in word and deed. May I bring only honest things to thee, to my parents, to my employer, to my teacher, and to my friends. May I not wish to profit by what would rob others. Make me honest with myself that I may not think more highly of myself than I ought. Help me to grow up a true man; through Jesus Christ our Lord. Amen.

FOR KINDNESS

O God, sometimes people need our love more than we know. Help us to remember to be kind and thoughtful always. For Jesus' sake. Amen.

FOR THE PRESENCE OF GOD

O God, most holy, be above me to protect me; underneath to support me; before me to guide me; behind me to forward me; within me to strengthen me; round about me to shield me. Be all things unto me. Amen.

Hear us, O Lord God, and be merciful unto us. Thou knowest our needs; teach us to feel them. Thou knowest our ignorance; teach us to pray. Thou knowest our weakness; teach us to look to thee for strength. Amen.

FOR PURITY

Eternal God, who hast taught us by thy Holy Word that our bodies are temples of thy Spirit: Keep us, we most humbly beseech thee, temperate and holy in thought, word, and deed, that at the last we, with all the pure in heart, may see thee and be made like unto thee in thy heavenly kingdom; through Jesus Christ our Lord. Amen.

Lord, help me to keep my thoughts pure, my words true, and my deeds kind, that alone or with others, I shall be at one with thee. Amen.

Righteous God, help me to be moderate in all things and never to waste my health and energy in pleasures which debase or destroy the powers thou givest me. Help me to keep my body and mind trained and fit, that they may be wholesome instruments of service and my soul may be free from remorse and despair. May I be in all my parts a worthy temple for thine indwelling and an honor to thy Name. Amen.

For Character and Spiritual Growth

FOR STRENGTH OF CHARACTER

O Lord, give me clean hands, clean words, and clean thoughts; help me to stand for the hard right against the easy wrong; save me from habits that harm; teach me to work as hard and play as fair in thy sight alone as if all the world saw; forgive me when I am unkind; and help me to forgive those who are unkind to me; keep me ready to help others at some cost to myself; send me chances to do a little good every day, and to grow more like Christ. Amen.

We ask thee, O Father, not for tasks equal to the powers we possess, but rather for powers equal to the tasks thou mayest set before us. Amen.

FOR RIGHTEOUSNESS

Grant to us, Lord, we beseech thee, the spirit to think and do always such things as are right; that we, who cannot do any thing that is good without thee, may by thee be enabled to live according to thy will; through Jesus Christ our Lord. Amen.

Our Father in heaven, we thank thee that in work and in play, in joy and in sorrow, thou art the friend and companion of us all. When we do wrong and grieve thee, thou art ready to forgive. When we do right, thou art glad.

May no hatred or envy dwell in our hearts. Keep our hands from selfish deeds and our lips from unkind words. Teach us to bring cheer to any who suffer and to share freely with those who are in need. So may we help thee, our Father, to bring peace, goodwill, and joy to all thy children. For Jesus' sake. Amen.

FOR TOLERANCE

Grant to me, Lord, I beseech thee, an open mind, ready to receive the truth and to act upon it. Show me that others have a right to their own opinions and help me to see their point of view. Give me grace to feel that I may be mistaken. Help me not to shut my mind to facts simply on the ground that I do not like them but ever to give the same weight to those which are unpleasant as I would give to those which are pleasant because they are in my favor. Open the eyes of my soul to see the truth. For Jesus' sake. Amen.

XXVII.
At Bedtime

For these glad hours
Of work and play,
For food and rest
At close of day,
We thank thee,
Heavenly Father. Amen.

Dear God, hear my evening prayer:
I thank thee for thy love and care,
I thank thee for this happy day,
For home and friends, for work and play.
Bless the ones I love tonight,
And keep us all till morning light. Amen.

Now
My work
And play

Are done,
I rest me
In thy care;
And while
I sleep,
Thy love
Will keep
Thy children everywhere. Amen.

Jesus, tender Shepherd, hear me,
Bless thy little lamb tonight,
Through the darkness be thou near me,
Keep me safe till morning light. Amen.

Father of all, who never dost sleep,
Keep watch over me while I rest.
I will put my trust in thee and not be afraid,
For no harm can come to me
When thou art my keeper.
Send thy peace and love into my heart
And fill my mind with happy thoughts.
Forgive all wrong in me,
And make me like Jesus;
For Jesus' sake. Amen.

O God, who lovest me all the day
And all the night;
Bless all I love,

At Bedtime

And keep them happy, keep them good;
And tomorrow
Make me obedient, unselfish, and kind;
For Jesus' sake. Amen.

   Dear Father in heaven,
Accept the good that I have done this day
And forgive the wrong.
Bless father and mother and all whom I love,
And keep us safely through the night;
For Jesus' sake. Amen.

   Gentle Jesus, meek and mild,
Look upon a little child;
Pity my simplicity,
Suffer me to come to thee.

Fain I would to thee be brought;
Dearest God, forbid it not:
Give me, dearest God, a place
In the kingdom of thy grace. Amen.

XXVIII.

In the Morning

For the new morning with its light,
For rest and shelter of the night,
We thank our heavenly Father.
For rest and food, for love and friends,
For everything his goodness sends,
We thank our heavenly Father. Amen.

Now I wake and see the light,
Thy love was with me through the night;
To thee I speak again and pray
That thou wilt lead me all the day. Amen.

O God, my loving Father,
Bless me at school today,
And help me to be attentive.
Bless me at home today,
And help me to be obedient.
Bless me at games today,
And help me to be unselfish.
Bless me at meals today,
And help me to be thankful.
For Jesus' sake. Amen.

In the Morning

Father, we thank thee for the night,
And for the pleasant morning light;
For rest and food and loving care,
And all that makes the day so fair. Amen.

Heavenly Father, hear my prayer;
Day and night I'm in thy care.
Look upon me from above,
Bless the home I dearly love.
Bless all those with whom I play;
Make me better every day. Amen.

Lord, bless thy little child today,
Make me good and kind, I pray. Amen.

Help us in all we do and say
To make more beautiful thy day. Amen.

We look to thee, dear Lord, and pray
That thou wilt guide us through this day.
From all wrongdoing keep us free.
May we thy loving children be. Amen.

XXIX.

At Mealtime

Father, we thank thee for this food,
For all thy love so great and good;
Feed all thy hungry ones today;
Bless all the world with us, we pray. Amen.

God is great, and God is good,
And we thank him for this food;
By his hand must all be fed;
Give us, O Lord, our daily bread. Amen.

We thank thee for this bread and meat
And all the good things which we eat;
Lord, may we strong and happy be,
And always good and true like thee. Amen.

XXX.
Of Praise

A CHILD'S CREED

I believe in God above.
I believe in Jesus' love.
I believe his Spirit, too,
Comes to teach me what to do.
I believe that I can be
True and loving, Lord, like thee. Amen.

IN PRAISE

Holy God, I come to worship thee.
Help me to be quiet, help me to be still.
Let me feel thy love around me,
Let me hear thy voice within me.
Fill me with praise, fill me with joy,
As I come to worship thee, O God. Amen.

Bless the Lord, O my soul, and all that is within me,
bless his holy Name. Bless the Lord, O my soul, and
forget not all his benefits. Amen.

XXXI.
For Others

FOR FAMILY AND OTHERS

O God, who art the loving father
Of all the people in the world,
I pray thee to take care of those I love
And those who love me,
Mother and father and ———.
Keep far away from them anything
That can hurt them,
And give them whatever is good for them.
Help us to love one another very much
And to love thee most of all;
Through Jesus Christ, our Lord. Amen.

FOR THE CHILDREN OF THE WORLD

Dear Father of the world family:
Please take care of all little children everywhere.
Keep them safe from danger
And help them to grow up strong and good. Amen.

XXXII.
Of Thanks

FOR HOME AND FAMILY

We thank thee, heavenly Father,
For our dear parents
Who love us and care for us each day.
Teach us to make them happy, to love them and obey
    them,
And to help them gladly with their work.
Forgive us for every disobedience
To our parents and to thee. Amen.

Great Father of all the world:
I thank thee for putting people in families
So that they can love and care for one another.
I thank thee for my home and for my family—
My mother and father, my brothers and sisters.
Please help us all to be loving
And thoughtful of one another,
So that our home may be full of joy. Amen.

FOR A NEW BABY

O God our Father:
I want to give thee
Special thanks for our baby.

Please show me ways
Of helping mother and father
To take care of *him*.

He is so sweet and tiny:
Please help me to be
Very gentle with *him*,
So that *he* may grow
Stronger and happier every day. Amen.

FOR GOD'S LOVE

I thank thee, God, our Father,
For the love thou hast put into the world:
The love of my mother and father,
Which was waiting for me when I came;
The love of the friends thou hast given me;
The love for others which thou hast put into my own
    heart;
And the love which I know thou hast for me. Amen.

FOR KIND PEOPLE

O God our Father: I thank thee
For all kind people.
Help me always myself to be
Kind and helpful to others, day by day. Amen.

FOR ANIMALS

O God our Father: I thank thee
For friendly animals and pets.

Of Thanks

Help me always to be kind
To all creatures, great and small. Amen.

FOR HAPPY TIMES

We thank thee, loving God, for happy times;
For our playmates and friends,
For our games and plays,
For our pets and trips;
We thank thee, loving God,
For all our happy times. Amen.

FOR BOOKS AND TOYS

I thank thee for my picture books,
I thank thee for my toys;
Please help me, God, to share them
With other girls and boys. Amen.

FOR THINGS WE ENJOY

Lord, we thank thee for this day,
For these hours of work and play,
For the shining sun above,
For thy great and tender love.
Help us, Lord, thy will to do;
Make us loving, kind, and true. Amen.

We thank thee then, O Father,
For all things bright and good;
The seedtime and the harvest,

Our life, our health, our food;
No gifts we have to offer
For all thy love imparts
But that which thou desirest,
Our humble, thankful hearts. Amen.

Thank thee, God, for sunny days
When we can run and play.
Thank thee, God, for rainy days
When all the sky is gray.
Thank thee, God, for home and friends,
For mother, father, too.
Thank thee, God, for helping us
In everything we do. Amen.

Thank God, who gives the harvest,
Sends wind and sun and rain,
To ripen sweet red apples
And fields of golden grain.
Thank God for friends and playtime,
For homes and loving care,
For schools and work and churches,
For chance to help and share.
Thank God for all the bounties
His love and kindness send.
Thank God, who gave us Jesus,
Our teacher, helper, friend. Amen.

XXXIII.

In Illness and Trouble

IN SICKNESS

O God, our Father,
The pain hurts very much.
Please help me to be brave,
But I know thou wilt understand
If I have to cry.
Please help me do
What the doctor says to do,
And not make it harder
For those who take care of me.
And help me, dear God,
To go to sleep
And be better in the morning. Amen.

AFTER ILLNESS

Loving Father: I am so glad
That I am now getting better
And have been able to get up today.
I thank thee for helping others
To make me better.
Please help me to grow stronger every day,

In Illness and Trouble

So that I may be able to do
All that thou hast planned for me. Amen.

WHEN HURT

O God,
Who seest me,
Make me brave,
For Jesus' sake. Amen.

WHEN AFRAID

O God, who art always with me
In the darkness and in the light;
Tell me now that thou art here;
For Jesus' sake. Amen.

WHEN IN TROUBLE

In the day of trouble
I will call upon thee, O God,
For thou wilt answer me.
God is my help and strength,
A very present help
In time of trouble.
Therefore, I will not fear. Amen.